DOLLS

A collector's guide

DOLLS

A collector's guide

Olivia Bristol

De Agostini *Editions*

This book is dedicated to Tim

Dolls *A collector's guide*
Olivia Bristol
De Agostini Editions

First published in Great Britain
by De Agostini Editions
Interpark House
7 Down Street
London W1Y 7DS

Distributed in the U.S.
by Stewart, Tabori & Chang,
a division of U.S. Media Holdings Inc.
575 Broadway
New York NY10012

Distributed in Canada
by General Publishing Company Ltd.
30 Lesmill Road, Don Mills
Ontario M3B 2T6

Library of Congress Catalog Card Number: 97-66895

Publishing Director: Frances Gertler
Senior Editor: Alison Macfarlane
Art Editor: Blânche-Adrienne Harper

ISBN: 1 86212 042 0

Printed in Spain

Contents

INTRODUCTION

Everyone has his or her own reason for wanting to collect dolls. Some wish to recapture and relive a happy childhood, others to experience something they were denied in their youth. Some simply like to see beautiful objects around them, fine clothes or funny faces to inspire their day or cheer them up.

For my part, I am fascinated by the idea of dolls, the children who played with them and the people who made them. What is the need for dolls? Why do so few little girls seem to play as intimately with them today, or has it always been like that? My aunts, now in their eighties, say they were "naughty little girls" and didn't care much for dolls, so maybe it was always so. Dolls tell so many stories. They reflect the tastes of the time and I find it interesting that what may appeal to an adult today may not necessarily have been attractive to a child at the time. Dolls also tell of changing fashions, not only of the dresses worn, but the looks, hairstyles, and figures, and it is the fact that this historical and social history can be learned through dolls that I find so absorbing.

And the story goes on. With the Far East replacing Germany as the major producer of dolls, and the wonderful dolls made by artists in Europe and the United States replacing the exquisite French bébés of the 1880s, people will continue to collect dolls as a reminder of times past and present, and the most expensive dolls will be kept in their cases to be looked at from afar.

RIGHT A fine wax-over-composition headed doll by Cuno and Otto Dressel, c.1890, dressed in an elaborate bridesmaid's gown of yellow and cream silk.

Starting a Doll Collection

Usually, doll collections start by accident. No conscious decision is taken, but a doll is bought on a whim, given as a present, or inherited and suddenly an interest is awakened. Once you are hooked it is a good idea to take stock of your feelings. What is it you like about dolls? How will your family react to you collecting them? How much money will you have to invest? How much room do you have to display your purchases? The answers to these questions are very important in helping you make a decision about your future collection. If you don't have much room, decide to collect smaller dolls, or even miniatures, and dolls' house dolls if space is really limited. If your funds are low, dolls made after the Second World War or out-of-fashion doll categories may be the answer. You could start collecting 1950s plastic dolls, or German composition, which have yet to become popular with collectors. Some cloth dolls can also be bought for relatively low prices. If your family doesn't like the thought of dolls around the house, you could collect paper dolls that can be stored flat in a drawer out of sight or in albums.

And of course, consider your personal taste. If your interest is in clothes of a particular period, limit your collecting to those dates, although be aware that the French lady dolls are among the most expensive dolls to buy. Some people collect only boy or men dolls, or black or Oriental dolls, and these too, make interesting collections. You could decide to collect in just one medium—for example, concentrating on wooden dolls or wax dolls. Or you may decide to focus on the products of one country, or even one maker. Obviously this will limit your choice, but will also present challenges to try and find the things you want and learn more about your chosen field.

Care is another deciding factor you should consider before you start collecting. Cloth dolls won't break, but they are very susceptible to moth holes, while an expensive bisque bébé or character doll will probably hold its value over the years, but if it is dropped be aware that its value will sink like a stone.

Join your local or national doll club which will not only keep you informed about what is going on in the doll world, but will put you in touch with other members and collectors. Visit their collections to get an idea of what

ABOVE German Oriental character dolls make an interesting collection. Shown here clockwise from top left are a Simon & Halbig mold 1129; a Kestner mold 243; an Armand Marseille mold 353; another Armand Marseille 353; and an Armand Marseille Ellar baby doll.

other people do. Go to doll shows, and visit dealers and auction houses. Ask your library for specialist books on the subject. Look and study as much as you can to decide what it is that most appeals to you.

Once you have some idea of what you would like to buy, you have several choices as to where you can go for your purchase. Auction houses now regularly hold sales of dolls, and although record-breaking prices hit the headlines, these are the exceptions, and you will be able to find reasonably priced dolls to suit your pocket. Even if you are not buying, go and view to see the range offered, or buy a catalog as a visual record of the possibilities available. A number of specialist dealers sell dolls through stores. Again, visit the store and browse through the selection, and remember to ask as many questions as you want. For those

RIGHT If you do not have much room to accommodate dolls, you can build up an interesting collection of miniatures. This group includes from left to right, a brown Ernst Heubach mold 399; an Armand Marseille copy; two cheeky mold 323 googly-eyed dolls by Armand Marseille; an anxious googly-eyed Gebrüder Heubach; and a lovely Armand Marseille Oriental baby with the Ellar tradename.

buying on a budget, antiques' markets and junk shops are an ideal hunting ground—and there is some excitement in the thought that you just might pick up a real bargain. Or visit flea markets. But be aware that you are more likely to find 1960s dolls than a beautiful Jumeau bébé! Dolls' magazines and clubs are also helpful, advertising the dolls of their members or subscribers.

For many people, collecting dolls is a case of opportunity. If they find a doll at the right price that they like, they buy it and it immediately becomes part of the family. This is a good way of collecting as you will have fun, and when and if you find a fabulous doll you can't resist or afford, then you will have some dolls to trade for it. Gradually your collection will take shape, reflecting your knowledge, character, interests, and personality

Never feel ashamed of collecting dolls. If they give you joy, then you will transmit that joy to others and make the world a happier place by your cheerful presence.

Insurance and documentation

It is important to make sure your dolls are adequately insured. Read your household policy to see if your dolls are covered. Usually you have to specify items over a certain value. If you have a few dolls, your insurance company may accept your own valuation if you can back it up with receipts or prices of similar dolls in catalogs or magazines. An insurance value is the figure you would have to pay to replace the item. It is therefore a retail figure not an auction price. Your insurance company may

ABOVE Many German manufacturers produced ethnic dolls, which make an interesting display when grouped together. From left to right here are a rare Ernst Heubach doll, mold 418; an Ernst Heubach mold 399; an Armand Marseille mold 341, and an Armand Marseille mold 362, all standing with a Roullet et Decamps clockwork skin-covered elephant.

ABOVE A rare set of early male paper dolls with twelve changes of costume, each outfit made up of all the garments as separate pieces of paper, published by S. & J. Fuller in 1811.

ABOVE Do not be afraid to buy dolls you like or find interesting, even if they do not fall into the usual areas. This weird group of dolls includes, from left to right, an English pedlar doll, c.1880, her head made from a dried apple; a rare papier-mâché-headed toy, c.1840; and a rather sanctimonious papier-mâché-headed Lutheran priest ready to hold something in his hands, c.1840.

insist you have a professionally written valuation and you will therefore need to contact an auction house or a reputable dealer to get this.

Whatever you choose to do, it is important to have records of your doll for your own use and for any future owner. Photograph your dolls, have a card for each doll with a detailed description, where and when you bought it, who you bought it from, and for how much. Detail any work that has been done to the doll, including changes of clothes or additions to the body. Keep anything you have had to replace, such as wigs, moth-eaten or damaged clothes, and so on in well-labeled plastic bags.

Fakes and reproductions

Care should always be taken when buying an antique doll. Until you are familiar with dolls and feel comfortable with your knowledge about them, seek professional help before purchasing. Specialist dealers and auction houses have reputations to uphold so they should give you sound advice. They will tell you if the doll has been restored, if the clothes are later than the doll, or if the body doesn't match the head. Many disasters happen at country flea markets in the half light of early dawn when a novice collector thinks he or she is getting a bargain from a dealer at the back of a van. He may look untidy but may well have fifty dolls like yours, newly imported and ready to unload!

Reproductions are not the same as fakes. They are copies of old dolls by modern makers and are usually marked, so confusion should not occur. But to help yourself recognize the "real" thing, study the fine antique dolls in museums and salerooms until you become familiar with the translucency of early bisque, and the painting details and imperfections of old dolls.

How to use this book and the price guide

Dolls in this book are listed chronologically by medium and each section is divided up into smaller collecting areas. There are sections on how to look after your doll, and at the back there is a gazetteer giving addresses of doll magazines, museums, and clubs. The prices given for each doll are intended as a guide only and represent the current auction house value at the time the book went to press. Prices vary from country to country, and ultimately collectors must decide the value for themselves. Condition will affect the value greatly—a doll that is in pristine condition with all its original clothes will be worth a great deal more than the same doll in poor condition. Availability also affects price. But remember, tastes change, and things quickly fall in and out of favor, so once again, buy a doll because you like it and want to own it.

ABOVE You may decide to collect the dolls of just one or two makers or from one country, giving yourself the opportunity to build up your expertise and knowlege. This group of German Käthe Kruse dolls is interesting because it represents the range the firm has produced over the years. From left to right are an unusual Snow White, c.1950; a pair of 1960s children in original clothes; and a rare baby Schlenkerchen from c.1922.

ABOVE Felt dolls, such as this 1930s Chad Valley girl, are very pretty and can often be bought at a relatively low cost. But beware of moth holes, which will devalue the doll enormously.

ABOVE Beware of fakes and marriages between parts that do not belong together. This doll has an SFBJ body, but the head is by Limoges.

A doll buyer's checklist

There are a number of questions you should ask yourself before buying a doll.

1 Do you like the doll, or are you just buying it because you think it is a bargain?

2 Are you happy that your knowledge is sufficient to evaluate the doll? If in doubt, seek professional assistance.

3 Does the body belong with the head? Familiarize yourself with marks and distinguishing features of different makers.

4 Is the price right?

5 Are the wig and body original or have they been replaced? Originals are always preferable.

6 Does the doll show evidence of restoration? Ask questions, and examine the doll carefully with a magnifying glass and flashlight if necessary.

7 Are the clothes original and in good condition, or if replacements, are they appropriate? Be careful about this: modern doll dressers are exceptionally gifted and many collectors have paid the price of an original costume for a dress that was really made only a few weeks beforehand.

8 Is the doll a good example of its type?

9 Does the doll have an interesting story?

10 Do you have enough space to display the doll?

A History of Dolls

Dolls have been made from ancient times in basic materials such as clay and wood. Sadly, few survive and those that do are only the finest examples that were made for the privileged rich, such as the pottery dolls found buried in Egyptian tombs.

It is known that Greek and Roman girls were given beautifully jointed and well-proportioned wooden figures adorned in gold and ivory bangles to present to the temple upon their marriage to symbolize the putting away of childish things. But again these were the possessions of the rich and we can only guess at the type of basic doll the poor may have owned and loved.

ABOVE A simple German mid-19th century peg wooden doll dressed in contemporary home-made printed clothes.

Although children must always have had dolls, there is no evidence of them again until the Middle Ages when wood-cuts were made portraying workers carving dolls out of wood. And some records report that terracotta dolls were being produced in Germany in the 15th century.

In England, 16th century portraits depict children holding elaborately dressed lady dolls, and primitive carved wooden stump dolls made from the 16th century until well into the 17th century survive in numbers today.

By the end of the 17th century, London-based doll-makers were well-established. They produced simply-made jointed wooden dolls with painted eyes, red cheeks, thin mouths, and quite often a beauty spot. This type of doll, with gradual variations, such as inset glass eyes, was made until the 1830s, when it was succeeded by the wooden and papier-mâché dolls being made in South Germany where wood-carving and the making of crèche figures were already long-established trades. 18th century German

RIGHT A German carved and painted wooden doll in original printed chintz sacque-back open robe and petticoat from c.1770.

dolls had more realistically carved heads, hands, and feet, and fine mortise and tenon jointing, but they appear to be rarer than English examples and little has been researched or written about them as yet.

Wax is another early material and was used for making dolls as long ago as the 1st century AD. By the Middle Ages it was used in profusion to make religious effigies for churches and chapels in such countries as Italy, Germany, and France. Many of the earliest wax examples that survive today are the small solid wax dolls made for dolls' houses in England and Germany in the 17th century, and some 18th century English wax lady dolls which are on display in the Victoria and Albert Museum and at the Bethnal Green Museum of Childhood in London, England. Munich was a center for wax doll production in the 18th century, making wax crèche figures dressed in elaborate costumes of the day rather than in the costumes they would actually have worn. It is interesting to note that perhaps the first baby dolls to have been made are the poured beeswax examples made in England at the turn of the 19th century. These are not only modeled as babies, but are dressed in long white robes and bonnets. Previously dolls had been dressed as adults.

Wax continued to be the preferred medium for dolls in England throughout the 19th and early 20th century,

LEFT Two 18th century wax dolls' house dolls with bead eyes dressed in their original clothes.

produced wooden dolls from the Grödnertal area and papier-mâché heads made in Sonneberg, but soon advertized dolls in other media as these became available.

By the 1840s china heads were being produced in Germany, France, and Denmark. However, their reign was shortlived, and in the 1860s china was superseded by bisque, which was particularly suited to doll production because of its life-like skin appearance.

In the United States during the early 19th century, where huge expansion and pioneering were taking place, dolls were either imported or home-made. But after the civil war in the 1860s, many small firms started to specialize in doll-making, mainly in New England and other northeastern states. Many interesting materials were used and ingenious patents taken out. Darrow in Connecticut used leather or rawhide; Joel Ellis and Mason & Taylor used wood and pewter; rubber heads were made in New York; papier-mâché heads were made by Ludwig Greiner and others in Philadelphia; and a number of small firms started by women made cloth dolls, with Izannah Walker obtaining a patent for her stiffened cloth heads in 1873.

with less expensive dolls being given papier-mâché heads dipped into hot liquid wax and the higher quality examples being made by pouring wax into a mold.

The great surge in doll production and acquisition came at the turn of the 19th century, when Germany began to publish its own *masterbuchs* (toy catalogs) in which many small firm's products were realistically illustrated and could be ordered by toy stores or by wholesalers. Not only could the buyer see in glorious watercolor what was offered, but he or she could buy dolls at prices that were significantly less than home-produced goods. They initially featured mass-

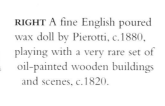

RIGHT A fine English poured wax doll by Pierotti, c.1880, playing with a very rare set of oil-painted wooden buildings and scenes, c.1820.

LEFT A c.1850 American lady with a gutta percha head on a cloth body with kid arms.

But it was in Paris in the 1880s that the peak of artistry in doll production was reached, and today the French bébé from this period is one of the most sought-after dolls. However, its demise was inevitable, as Germany went on to produce a vast array of bisque dolls which were much less expensive than their French counterparts. Bisque dolls continued to be popular right up until the outbreak of the Second World War in 1939, and this explains why they represent most of the antique dolls that appear on the market today.

1909 was a huge turning point in the doll world, when beauty, or the standard "dolly" look was to give way to realism with the introduction of the bisque character doll by Kämmer & Reinhardt. Others soon followed suit. Käthe Kruse brought out her child-like cloth Doll 1 in 1910; in 1912 the realistic Munich Art Dolls were exhib-

ited; and at the same time Steiff, the soft toy makers, were producing a wide variety of dolls closely modeled on a myriad of adults, children, and comic characters.

In the 1920s the Italian firm of Lenci designed a huge range of beautifully-dressed cloth child dolls, and firms in England, France, Germany, and the United States were constantly introducing new designs using cloth, composition, and celluloid. Many smaller firms copied successful designs of others and it is important to make sure you have an example by one of the better makers.

After the Second World War plastics came into their own, with the hard plastics of the 1940s being followed by rubber, foam rubber, and vinyl in the 1950s and 1960s, heralding a time of inexpensive, mass-market dolls. Yet today more and more doll makers are drawing on traditional materials, with modern doll artists using anything

LEFT An American Izannah Walker cloth doll with an oil painted face and a typically naive mid-19th century hairstyle.

RIGHT An extremely interesting François Gaultier lady doll from 1877 wearing a dress and hat designed by Madam Goubaud, editor of *Myra's Journal of Dress and Fashion*, who also produced it as a colored tissue paper pattern dress front.

FAR RIGHT A pretty Jules Nicolas Steiner Figure A bébé, one of the most frequently found Steiner molds, with straight wrists and a body stamped "Le Petit Parisien Bébé Steiner."

from wood and cloth to high quality porcelain to produce what may become the collectibles of tomorrow.

There are fashions in doll collecting as in everything else. Early collectors favored historical dolls, chinas, waxes, and woodens. In the early 1970s French bébés and wax dolls were desirable. During the 1980s character dolls rose in popularity and in the 1990s it is the French bébés again and rare German characters that are most sought-after.

Collectors are wise to not necessarily follow fashion but to collect what they find most appealing. Then they can create trends for the future while still enjoying their collection today.

ABOVE A typical German bisque character doll, mold 116A, made by Simon & Halbig for Känmer & Reinhardt.

ABOVE A Käthe Kruse doll 1 dressed as a boy, but wearing someone else's trousers!

RIGHT A Vogue company hard plastic Ginny, called "Wet, Combed, Curled and Set," dating to 1952. She comes complete with wardrobe and instructions on how to dress her and wash and blow-dry her hair.

RIGHT A very rare Lenci portrait doll modeled as Rudolph Valentino dressed as "The Sheik" in orginal jodpurs and knee-length leather boots and with carved and painted wooden dagger and pistol, c.1927.

WOODEN DOLLS

Wood was one of the earliest materials used in toy-making, with some dolls dating from ancient times. In England, stump dolls made in the 16th and 17th centuries survive in small quantities, but they lack the esthetic appeal of other dolls and are usually bought by collectors of folk art. By the end of the 17th century more elaborate jointed dolls, their heads covered in gesso and oil paint, were being produced by specialist makers in London who are unidentifiable today. The dolls were probably sold dressed and if the clothes survive they are extremely well-fitted and reflect the fashions of the day.

By the end of the 18th century, wooden dolls were being made in large quantities in England and Germany, with the Grödnertal area producing a wide range of dolls known today as peg woodens or Grödnertals. From the beginning of the 18th century to the early 20th realistic crèche figures were also being carved. America made some interesting wooden dolls, including early country primitives and the spring-jointed examples made from 1911 in Philadelphia by Albert Schoenhut.

The earliest wooden dolls are very rare and expensive but peg woodens and the more simply-carved examples can still be bought for modest sums today.

LEFT (left to right) A carved and painted early Bavarian wooden doll, c.1820; a turned wood doll with elastic jointing modeled as Pinnochio (not the Disney version); another turned wood painted figure; and an early 19th century English wooden doll.

RIGHT An early 20th century wooden character doll by Albert Schoenhut.

English Wood

The first English wooden dolls were very simple carved affairs, but they became increasingly sophisticated during the 17th and 18th centuries. They were carved from a single piece of wood coated with a gesso primer and then painted details were added. The bodies were dressed in tightly-fitting fashionable clothes, usually made from scraps of silk, with quilted cotton petticoats, stays, and linen shifts, and wigs of brown human hair were nailed to their heads. The more expensive dolls had carved ears, noses, and chins; the less expensive ones were given very crudely carved limbs linked by nails to the body with pieces of leather or linen. Sometimes even breasts were carved. The foremost maker, whose name, like that of so many early doll-making families, is unknown (but judging by the style of the original clothes was probably operating in the 18th century), carved dolls with beautiful legs and arms with ball and hinge joints at the shoulder and elbow and with snugly fitting hips and knees.

RIGHT Wooden dolls from the 17th century are extremely rare and as they are almost priceless today, are beyond the realms of most collectors' pockets. However, it is interesting to look at the skill and craftsmanship involved and to marvel at how something so old and fragile can have survived in such excellent condition. Dating from c.1680, this carved doll is an outstanding example. She is still wearing her original green brocade bodice and shows little evidence of damage. Particularly interesting is her very thin waist, carved to fit the tight dresses of the times and very different from the bodies of the 19th century examples on the next page. She has beautifully carved hands and fine fingers, and her short sleeves reveal the simple hinge jointing at her elbows. Despite her thin waist, she shares many characteristics of the later examples, including rouged cheeks, fine eyebrows, and a round face.
Height: (13in) 33cm
Value: $60,000-$90,000

LEFT The torso and head of early English wooden dolls were turned on a lathe and carved, then coated in a layer of gesso and painted; the close-up of this doll from c.1770 shows in detail the delicate carving of these early dolls. Although she now shows signs of wear—she has lost her eyebrows, and the paint is chipped on her nose, lips, and chin— she was originally a high-quality doll, with intricately carved ears, a nailed-on wig, long neck, pronounced chin, and well-painted face.
Height: 20in (51cm)
Value: $8,000-15,000

RIGHT This is a simpler and less expensive version of the doll below, but she is still highly desirable because she is in such good condition and wearing her original clothes. Her wig of human hair is intact, and she still has the remains of a silk rosette. Her severe expression, stitched eyebrows and eyelashes, and uncompromising long, straight mouth are all unrubbed. She has the typically short neck and sloping shoulders of these mid-18th century dolls, with short arms that taper into roughly carved hands that here still wear the remnants of muslin mittens. Other typical features include her red cheeks and thin mouth.
Height: 8in (20cm)
Value: $2,500-4,000

LEFT From the end of the 18th century the construction of English wooden dolls was slightly simpler than for earlier dolls, although the principles were the same. This was probably because English toy-makers had to try and lower their prices to compete with the large quantities of attractive German dolls that were being imported into the country from the Grödnertal area (see p.21). This demure lady from 1815 is wearing her original clothes which are typical of the fashions of the day.
Height: 20in (51cm)
Value: $2,500-4,000

RIGHT This magnificent English turned and carved wood doll was probably made by the finest 18th century doll-maker. She has delicate features with the slightly downcast inset glass eyes that were fashionable in the 18th century, and looks as though she is smiling to herself. Her entire body is painted in a pale flesh tone over the gesso primer and she has smooth well-fitting joints at the hip and knee and ball and groove joints at the shoulder and elbow. Her hands are well-carved with definite thumbs and fingers, designed so that she could actually hold something. She was probably made c.1780, although the cape she is wearing is later.
Height: 22in (55cm)
Value: $24,000-30,000

Early German

Because Germany already had a long history of wood carving—making crèche and religious figures for its Catholic churches—when it started to make hand-carved dolls at the turn of the 18th century, they were usually of superior quality to English ones. The faces are more detailed and the bodies and limbs are beautifully shaped and jointed, often with ball and tenons at the joints, and carved legs and shoes rather than the rudimentary "hoof" of many English dolls. They also paid more attention to fine details, painting on elaborate stockings, colored heels, and gold buckles.

LEFT This lovely finely carved and jointed South German wooden doll is wearing the local costume that was fashionable for upper class women in c.1765. A portrait in the Germanische National Museum in Nuremburg shows a girl wearing the same style of hooded jacket with its full skirt. Her padded cotton under-petticoat is typical of those worn by 18th century women to keep the cold at bay. Her delicately carved hands and accurate proportions reflect the typical high standard of these early German dolls. She is wearing her original wig, simply plaited down her back, but unfortunately, her original paintwork has worn away on her extremities, revealing the wood. Undressed, the much more sophisticated detail of these earlier dolls can be seen, with ball joints that enable them to move in all directions. Her small breasts have faintly indicated nipples, presumably to denote a young girl rather than an adult. Her shoes are very elegant, with gray heels and with the remains of gold buckles painted on the tops. Her stockings also have white detailing at the side to represent embroidered clocks.
Height: 14½in (37cm)
Value: $3,000-$4,000

Grödnertals

By the 19th century, Germany was mass-producing charming high-quality wooden dolls, known as Grödnertals after the Groden valley region in Southern Germany where many of them were made. The dolls were well-made and well-jointed, often with carved hair rather than wigs and sometimes with carved and painted bodices and simpler hands and feet with red, blue or green slippers painted on their legs. *Biberach's masterbuch* was produced to illustrate the dolls and toys available from Germany in 1804. Agents were then able to show clients clearly what was available and the organisation of home workers improved to such an extent that inexpensive dolls could be ordered in quantity by toy shops throughout Europe and the United States.

RIGHT A number of Grödnertals were made as pedlar dolls. This unfortunate lady has dropped her basket, displaying all her exquisitely made wares. Pedlar dolls were made in England from the 1830s to the 1860s in a number of different materials, including wax, composition, kid, bisque and even with dried apple heads (see p.51). This example is wearing the typical early costume of a red-hooded cape, printed dress and apron.
Height: 25.5cm (10in)
Value: £600-800

ABOVE This 1830s Grödnertal has the typical carved yellow comb found on these dolls, together with the characteristic grey curls on her cheeks and the wire loops for her earrings. She is dressed as a Welsh woman in a boldly checked wool. Grödnertals were usually sold without clothes, apart from their painted slippers. Their appeal was in the fact that they were so inexpensive that middle and upper class children could afford to buy them with their pocket money and dress them in remnants from the needlework cupboard.
Height: 30.5cm (12in)
Value: £180-250

ABOVE Queen Victoria loved Grödnertal dolls. She bought 132 of them which she and her governess, Baroness Lehzen, dressed. They gave them names, sometimes of imaginary aristocratic pedigrees, or from the ballet or the latest plays. They have survived with their original clothes and are now in the Museum of London.
This page from *Queen Victoria's Dolls*, published in 1894, is a lovely record of the dolls.
Value: £100-150

Peg Woodens

By the end of the 1890s, the high-quality Grödnertal dolls of the early 1800s had deteriorated into cheaply made peg woodens, many of which were mass-produced for the Colonies. These dolls have crude, barely-finished limbs attached with pegs at the joint, which are easily broken. They are painted only at the visible parts, in white, with a suggestion of a red shoe at the end of shapeless legs. Their faces are their endearing feature, with a variety of amusing expressions. Because they were painted by hand at extreme speed, by unskilled workers or child labor, it is their differences that give them their appeal.

LEFT From the largest to the smallest, each peg wooden had the same simple construction. Being such perfect pocket money toys, and so easy to dress in numerous outfits, the dolls were a favorite of many children. But because they were mass-produced and are so widely available today, only those with a special feature or still in their original home-made clothes are truly collectible. Here, the smaller dolls are early; the larger ones are later. They would be worth more if they were dressed. Height: 1¼in-12in (3-30.5cm) Value: small dolls $50-100; large dolls $15-25

ABOVE The fact that this doll has carved plaits suggests it was made in the Italian toy-making village of Ortesei, as dolls with similar hairstyles appear in an Ortesei catalog. Typical features include the simply-constructed peg joints, limbs painted only from the elbows and knees, and home-made clothes. Height: 10in (25.4cm) Value: $50-75

ABOVE Possibly because of their simple construction and the fact that they could be made to pose, peg woodens were very popular with authors and illustrators. These pages from *Me and Catharine Susan* by Kathleen Ainslie show the typical peg woodens in childrens' story books, and are modeled very closely on the originals. Value: $50-60

Crèche Figures

It has long been the tradition in Catholic countries to display the nativity scene at Christmas time. The figures included not only the Holy Family and the stable, but also the shepherds, wise men, angels, and indeed the whole of Bethlehem from its highest to the lowest. Various materials were used. Beautifully-carved and painted wooden figures from Germany have been admired for centuries. In Naples, intricately detailed heads are usually of terracotta and these dolls, which have survived in large numbers, represent an elaborate study of life in Southern Italy well into the 19th century. Because of their variety and the fact that they are relatively inexpensive, crèche figures provide a good opportunity to collect an early doll.

ABOVE This delightful 19th century local village character is probably Neopolitan because, although he has finely-carved hands and legs, he has a low-fired ceramic head. His clothes are all original and he is dressed as a laborer, possibly as one of the shepherds, with his knapsack over his shoulder and typically simple footwear.
Height: 10in (25.4cm)
Value: $400–700

ABOVE Judging by the expression of this Neopolitan crèche figure, it is very likely he was intended to represent the village idiot—although it could simply be that he has just been surprised by the visit of the angel Gabriel! He has a wire body covered in tow, realistic limbs, and is dressed as a shepherd.
Height: 8½in (21.5cm)
Value: $350–600

ABOVE The fact that this magnificent lady from c.1820 is beautifully carved and dressed suggests that she was one of the well-to-do figures of the town: even her shoes look expensive! She has beautifully arranged carved hair decorated with horizontal bands and is wearing silk clothes that reflect her wealth.
Height: 22½in (57cm)
Value: $500–700

A. Schoenhut & Co.

Albert Schoenhut moved to Philadelphia from Germany in 1866. In 1911 he patented his design for carved wooden dolls with wire spring-jointed bodies that could move at the neck, shoulders, elbows, wrists, hips, knees, and ankles. He wanted to produce a robust doll that could withstand heavy play, but as a result his dolls are not very cuddly. They had heat-pressed heads with facial details carved by hand, painted features, often with intaglio eyes, and carved hair or mohair wigs. Production of wood dolls ceased by 1930; dolls in good condition are sought-after today.

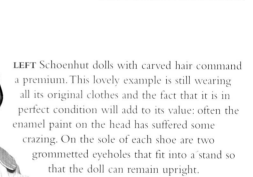

RIGHT Adolph Graziano was one of Schoenhut's earliest wood carvers, making heads such as this one for a short period in 1911. He also carved distinctive hairstyles, sometimes adding a ribbon or bow. His designs are the most desirable of Schoenhut's dolls.
Height: 15in (38cm)
Value: $2,200–3,000

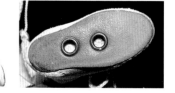

LEFT Schoenhut dolls with carved hair command a premium. This lovely example is still wearing all its original clothes and the fact that it is in perfect condition will add to its value: often the enamel paint on the head has suffered some crazing. On the sole of each shoe are two grommetted eyeholes that fit into a stand so that the doll can remain upright.
Height: 19in (48cm)
Value: $1,800–2,800

ABOVE Albert Schoenhut produced a variety of different molds; shown here are a typical pouty face doll of the 1920s (on the right) and the less popular 1930s dolly face (on the left), standing with a wooden horse also made by the company.
Height: left 16in (40.5cm); right 19in (48cm)
Value: left $600–800; right $900–1,800

Russian Wood

In Russia, wooden dolls have been recorded as having been made since the 14th century, when wooden religious figures were carved for pilgrims visiting monasteries. Carved toy troika and carriages with horses and figures were made, and simple, painted wooden dolls with no arms and no articulation. Today, Russia is probably most famous for its traditional *Matryoshka* or Nesting Dolls, still in production. Often, the outermost doll is a woman, sometimes romantically said to represent Mother Russia.

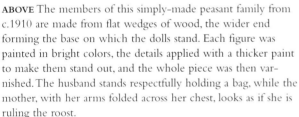

RIGHT This type of doll, crudely carved from a triangular piece of wood, has been made in Russia since the early 19th century. The bright painted decoration is often worn, because simple water-soluble poster paints were used.
Height: 10½in (26.5cm)
Value: $125–250

ABOVE The members of this simply-made peasant family from c.1910 are made from flat wedges of wood, the wider end forming the base on which the dolls stand. Each figure was painted in bright colors, the details applied with a thicker paint to make them stand out, and the whole piece was then varnished. The husband stands respectfully holding a bag, while the mother, with her arms folded across her chest, looks as if she is ruling the roost.
Height: largest doll 9in (23.5cm)
Value: $250–400 the set

RIGHT This set of dolls from c.1910 is particularly well-made. Typically, the mother is the largest doll, followed by her husband and children. She is clutching a pig, suggesting the family's peasant lifestyle.
Height: largest doll 8½in (21.5cm)
Value: $100–200 the set

Chinese Wood

In China in the early 20th century, carved wooden dolls were made in missions set up to save children, slave girls, and young widows from destitution. In 1901, a Shanghai sanctuary called the Door of Hope opened. Others followed, operating as part of the mission. The girls were taught to read and write as well as sew dolls' costumes. Chinese dolls are interesting to collect because of the variety of different head carvings and costumes and because they reflect the social history of China at the start of the 20th century.

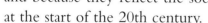

ABOVE This c.1905 Shanghai Door of Hope doll is dressed as a mandarin, with his badge of office on his tunic. His head is well-carved and realistic; Canton dolls had composition heads and are far less desirable.
Height: 12in (30.5cm)
Value: $350–600

ABOVE The fact that this doll has unbound feet suggests she was made after 1911, when the binding of feet was made illegal, or that she is from North China, where binding was not the custom.
Height: 12in (30.5cm)
Value: $350–600

RIGHT This c.1920s *amah*, or nurse, is carrying her well-clad charge on her back. A later example, she does not display the high quality of the earlier dolls that were so finely-carved that only their lips, eyes, hair, and eyebrows were painted on the wood. Typically, she is in good condition; the dolls were initially made for display and have not been damaged through play.
Height: 10½in (26.5cm)
Value: $450–750

Miscellaneous Wood

A lot of simply-carved and inexpensive wooden dolls exist, many of them home-made. From the 16th century oak 'stump' dolls were produced in England and Germany. These are usually small and crudely carved out of a single piece of wood as a solid figure with an indication of a costume and hairstyle that can help to date them. Over the years they have gained a soft patina and are lovely to hold, although their faces cannot be described as pretty. In the 19th century American fathers would turn to wood if no other doll was available for their child. Fascinating examples survive, some with leather pieces nailed to the wood to create joints. Again, these dolls are not very pretty, but there is a lot of interest in them, particularly in the United States and among folk art collectors. Although they are very rare, their prices are relatively low.

ABOVE Not all the dolls made in the 19th century were as sophisticated as those featured in this chapter. Dolls carved from a single piece of wood were produced both in England and Germany at this time. This oak doll, probably dating to c.1860, was possibly made as part of a set of skittles. She has carved features, including elaborate ringlets, and a painted jacket.
Height: 10in (25.4cm)
Value: $100–300

ABOVE This Swiss wooden shoulder head from 1930s is very well-carved, with painted hair and features. These heads and whole dolls were made between the First and Second World Wars, some with interesting, typically Swiss hairstyles. On whole dolls the bodies were carved and well-jointed, usually at the neck, shoulders, elbows, hips, and knees.
Height: 3½in (9cm)
Value: $100–200

ABOVE Despite being known as *bébés tout-en-bois*, these rather ugly all-wood baby dolls were made in Germany in the 1890s by such firms as Schilling and Cuno and Otto Dressel. The carving is always very similar with painted hair and stationary glass eyes. This doll is unusual because it has an open mouth possibly ready for a bottle or dummy whereas most have closed mouths.
Height: 15in (38cm)
Value: $350–600

ABOVE Simple wooden dolls, such as this example, were produced for Dryads Handicrafts in England in the 1950s and sold with dress patterns for making their clothes. The head and torso of this girl are of turned wood and the shoulders and hips are jointed with metal pins. Some earlier examples had celluloid slips at the joints, allowing more movement.
Height: 11in (28cm)
Value: $20–30

PAPIER-MÂCHÉ AND COMPOSITION DOLLS

Papier-mâché dolls existed but were not made in quantity until the early 19th century. The French made crude "carton-head" dolls, brightly painted and elaborately dressed in the latest Paris fashions. English dolls, also crudely molded, were dipped in wax. In Germany the medium was developed to its full potential: in dolls with elaborate molded hairstyles, kid bodies, and turned wood limbs. Many heads were exported to France and were put on pink kid bodies similar to those on French lady dolls. Papier-mâché heads were also made in the United States, notably in Philadelphia by makers such as Ludwig Greiner.

Composition, a compound with more wood fiber than papier-mâché, was commercially developed for doll making in the last quarter of the 19th century. Made in ever-greater quantities well into the 20th century, unless these dolls are in exceptional condition or have some interesting feature, their values are not excessively high.

LEFT (left to right) An American Horsman black Baby Bumps, c.1912; a Chinese composition girl, c.1960; a German papier-mâché girl, c.1850; a Sonneberg papier-mâché doll, c.1850; and a very rare tightrope walking doll by Jules Nicolas Steiner, c.1870.
RIGHT A Japanese couple made by Goya Hirata in the 1920s.

German Papier-Mâché

Papier-mâché was used extensively in the 18th and early 19th centuries to make furniture and small items. In the 1820s German doll makers began to adopt the medium for dolls' heads and continued to use it for their dolls until the 1860s. *Masterbuchs* from the 1840s show the great range of styles they produced and are a useful source of reference when buying the dolls. Most of the heads were sold with a white kid body and simply turned and painted wooden arms, colored paper bands covering the joints between the wood and the kid. A number of the heads were exported without bodies and as a result many other types of body can be found. Heads bought by the French often have a pink kid gusseted body, similar in construction to those of their later bisque and china-headed fashionable dolls (see p.65), and may also have been dressed in France, as they can be found wearing elaborate sewn-on French provincial costumes.

This well-worn and rather dirty lady was made in 1834 and sports the typical exaggerated curls and top-knot of the period. Papier-mâché dolls are notoriously easy to damage as they were painted in tempera and water-soluble varnishes, both of which wash off easily, but a fine example such as this is still desirable.
Height: 27in (68.5cm)
Value: $800–1,500

RIGHT Papier-mâché shoulder heads with real hair wigs are generally more desirable than those with molded hair. It is rare to find the original hair still in such a perfect style as this 1830s example, which even has the original artificial flower arrangement. She has inset glass eyes, well-carved painted wooden hands, and a charming cotton lawn summer dress of the period; peeping below are the typical painted slippers of these dolls.
Height: 22in (55cm)
Value: $1,500–2,000

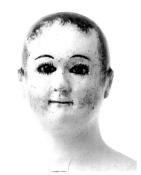

LEFT This is a typical, high-quality shoulder head with fine modeling and painting. Special features include the inset glass eyes rather than the painted ones of less expensive examples, and the elaborate styling of her hair.
Height: head only
Value: $800–1,200

ABOVE The black painted pate of this doll from the 1860s was once covered with an elaborate human hair wig, which, sadly, is now missing except for a few strands. This will reduce the value, as it would be difficult to find a suitable well-made replacement wig.
Height: 16in (40.5cm)
Value: $500–800

ABOVE Papier-mâché shoulder heads modeled as men are very rare. This 1840s doll's head has short hair with brush strokes indicating curls swept forward toward the temples, commonly known as "*coups de vent*." The head is very light and shows the cracking signs typical of papier-mâché; the paint and varnish are also worn, and there is evidence of some re-touching.
Height: head only
Value: $800–1,200

RIGHT Early dolls such as this example from the 1820s wore the Empire hairstyles reminiscent of Greece and Rome that were popular among women at the beginning of the 19th century. Although the head is German, it is likely that it was exported to England to have a body attached: its body is made of cloth with pink kid arms, very similar to those of English wax dolls of the period (see p.46).
Height: 16in (40.5cm)
Value: $800–1,500

LEFT Similar papier-mâché heads to this unusual man in a turban appear in the German doll catalogs of the 1840s. He has the typical wooden limbs and painted slippers of the female dolls of this time. Although his shirt has been replaced, he is still wearing his original trousers. He is a very rare doll, modeled as a Turk, and is very desirable.
Height: 10in (25.4cm)
Value: $700-1,200

ABOVE This lady is typical of the papier-mâché dolls made for export in Sonneburg, Germany, in the 1840s. Typical features include the simply-molded hairstyle, wooden limbs attached to a kid body with blue paper bands to conceal the joints, a slim body, and painted facial details
Height: 12in (30.5cm)
Value: $400-1,200

FRENCH *CARTON* DOLLS

French papier-mâché dolls are very rare as *carton* was used mainly to produce display models for the fashion stores of the time. The face of this 1820s doll is less realistic than that of her German counterparts, but she is more finely-made, with inset glass eyes, a beautifully-sewn kid body, and original silk dress.
Height: 20in (51cm)
Value: $2,000-3,000

American Papier-Mâché

In the early 19th century Germany exported papier-mâché heads to the United States, where cloth bodies were attached to them, but by the 1850s American manufacturers had started to make the heads themselves. Ludwig Greiner's patent of 1858 seems to be the first record of American-made papier-mâché dolls, although it is probable that he was experimenting and creating heads before he lodged his patent. Philadelphia was an important center and was home not only to Ludwig Greiner, but also to a number of other manufacturers, including Judge and Early, the Knell brothers, and Philip Lerch. They did not produce the variety of hairstyles found on earlier German heads, possibly because women's hairstyles in the United States during the 1850s and 1860s were not as elaborate and fanciful as those of European women from 1800 to 1840 when the German heads were made. These early American dolls are scarce today, and are a very important element in the history of doll-making in the United States.

ABOVE This commercially-made mid-19th century papier-mâché/composition doll was introduced to her current owner with the words "This is Judy. She steals children." She is very similar to the puppet Judy in the children's show *Punch and Judy*, especially in her nose, open mouth, and the frill under her bonnet. Her "stolen" children are small German bisques. Unique dolls such as this are difficult to value.
Height: 18in (46cm)
Value: $4,000+

LEFT This unmarked papier-mâché shoulder head lady from c.1850 has 16 deeply cut sausage curls, which are molded close to her head and forward onto her cheeks, giving her face a narrow look. Her homespun cloth body has leather arms, which is a typical combination, and she is wearing a period dress and shoes.
Height: 22in (55cm)
Value: $1,800-2,200

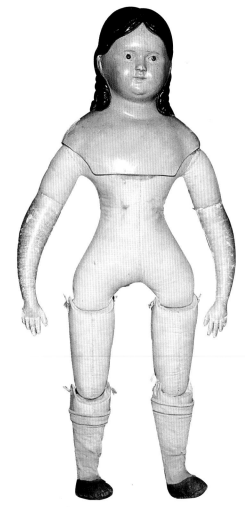

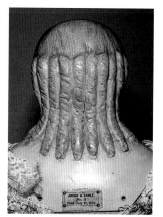

ABOVE Edward S. Judge was one of the many toy makers in Philadelphia. He was granted patents for papier-mâché heads in 1868 and 1875. His mark bears the name of Early but the two's relationship is unclear. This doll's elegant hairstyle of molded, long blond curls falling gracefully over her shoulders is belied by the simplicity of the front of the hair, pulled back severely from her face and held in place by an Alice band.
Height: 24in (61cm)
Value: $3,000–3,500

ABOVE and LEFT The head of this papier-mâché doll is attached to a cloth body patented by Sarah Robinson in 1883. It has well-articulated cloth joints that move by means of cords through the upper section attached to washers or buttons on the outside of the limbs. The arms are leather with separate fingers. Her nicely-molded hair is particularly attractive, with tight ringlets, reflecting the hairstyles of the day.
Height: 21in (53cm)
Value: $2,200–2,800

LEFT and ABOVE Philip Lerch made dolls' heads from 1866 until the 1870s. The Lerch & Klag label appears to date from the 1870s, although little is known about Mr Klag. Notice how the head is in the style of the 1860s when Alice bands were fashionable.
Height: 16½in (42cm)
Value: $2,500–3,500

LEFT Greiner heads were usually made with brown painted eyes; the blue eyes of this example are rarer. Other features are almost identical to the dolls on the left, apart from the rolled curls of hair coming from her center parting and across her temples.
Height: 24in (61cm)
Value: $1,200–1,500

ABOVE Ludwig Greiner was a German doll-maker who emigrated to the United States and produced dolls under his name from 1840 until 1874 and then with his sons until 1883. He gained his first patent for papier-mâché heads in 1858 and dolls from this time are marked with the date of the patent. This example is one of his earliest dolls, probably made at around the time the patent was granted, and is simply stamped "patent head." Typically, the doll has molded black hair parted in the center.
Height: 24in (61cm)
Value: $4,000–4,500

ABOVE The hairstyles of Greiner's dolls were very similar to those found on German shoulder heads of the day (see p.95). This slightly later example has a short windblown hairstyle, which is almost masculine in its appearance. Her label has the added word "improved," even though the patent is still the 1858 one. Her head is typically large in proportion to her body, which is apparent in the group shot of the dolls, below right.
Height: 21in (53cm)
Value: $1,800–2,500

RIGHT The group shot of the dolls in this section shows their various sizes and body-shapes. When collecting dolls, it is always nice to be able to display dolls of the same type together in this way.

German Composition

One of the frequently overlooked categories of dolls are the composition-headed examples made in Germany between the 1860s and the end of the century. As inexpensive toys, many suffered in hard play and were discarded. They are generally unmarked, so attribution is difficult. Often worn or damaged, good examples are scarce, but are not highly regarded. Thus, an interesting collection can be built for a small investment. Firms such as Cuno and Otto Dressel, Kestner, and Schilling made composition heads for the less expensive end of the market and if found with their original paint these are often as pretty as their bisque sisters. They usually have stationary glass eyes, a stuffed body with a squeaker, and well-modeled composition limbs. Some have beautiful, brightly colored boots. Avoid poor quality dolls, especially if redressed, but otherwise they offer the chance to own an unusual antique doll for a fraction of the cost of bisque examples.

LEFT Examples of this composition-headed soldier doll appear in an illustrated *Masterbuch* of the 1860s, where he is featured in a group with other soldiers standing around a toy cannon. He is wearing the popular Zouave costume with baggy knee breeches and carries a wooden water barrel. Each soldier has a back pack with a rolled-up bed roll. The bodies are of well-jointed wire, allowing them to be placed in any number of positions, including running, as one foot is held firmly in place by a wooden peg in the base, making them the ideal 19th century G I Joe toy for boys. They have unpainted wood hands and painted composition legs.
Height: 9in (23.5cm)
Value: $250-400

LEFT This composition clown with cloth body and felt clothes was advertised in the German Universal Toy Catalog of 1926. He is a typical example of the type of mass-produced composition doll with painted features made at the time. He wears a simple, inexpensive felt clown's outfit.
Height: 17in (43cm)
Value: $75-125

THINGS TO LOOK FOR:

• original painting and varnish
• absence of chips, cracks, crazing, "lifting," or flaking
• clean and undamaged body
• glass eyes
• original clothes: most composition dolls had factory or store-made clothes and these are an important part of the doll
• unusual molds and mid-19th-century toys incorporating composition figures

ABOVE Few composition shoulder heads survive in the excellent condition of this all-original example from the 1880s, but despite her rarity, she is still considerably less expensive than her bisque-headed counterparts. Frequently, the varnish has rubbed or washed off, but here it survives in near-perfect condition.
Height: 11in (27.5cm)
Value: $250-400

ABOVE Many inexpensive, poor-quality composition dolls were made that today are of little interest to the collector. This example, probably from the 1930s, is wearing home-made clothes and her construction and features have little visual appeal or technical merit when compared with those of the fine example on the left.
Height:12in (30.5cm)
Value: $50-100

LEFT The Munich Art Doll movement produced dolls from 1912 designed by a number of different artists, including most famously Paul Vogelsanger and Marian Kaulitz. This composition-headed doll has an oil-painted character face and modeling similar to that of the Kämmer and Reinhardt mold 101 doll, Marie. Her body is also of composition, jointed in a similar style to that of the bisque-headed dolls made in Germany.
Height: 19in (48cm)
Value: $2,200-3,500

American Composition

There were many small American companies making composition-headed dolls during the first half of the 20th century and quality therefore varies considerably. Edward Imeson Horsman was one of the first to make composition doll heads, producing perhaps most famously the Campbell Kids for the Campbell soup company. Other major makers of composition dolls are Fleischaker & Baum (trading under the name of EFFanBEE) who made beautifully designed "Mama" dolls with cloth bodies, composition limbs, and voice boxes; the Cameo Doll Company, who based their dolls on the well-known characters created by, among others, Joseph L. Kallus, Rose O'Neill, and Jack Collins; the American Character Doll Company; and Madame Alexander. The original clothes and the condition of composition dolls are extremely important, as composition deteriorates easily and the clothes form a large part of the value of the doll.

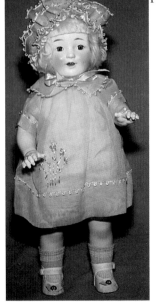

LEFT New York-based E.I. Horsman was one of the earliest manufacturers of composition-headed dolls, making the first examples in 1909 when so many German makers were starting to produce character faces. Many of the dolls are marked "E.I.H. Co.," sometimes with the date and the copyright sign. Their "Mama" dolls had composition heads, arms, and legs, sleeping eyes, and stuffed bodies containing gravity-operated voice boxes activated by turning the doll upside down. This is a particularly desirable doll because she is in perfect condition, is still in her original box, and is wearing her original embroidered organdy dress, bonnet, and socks.
Height: 16in (40.5cm)
Value: $600–900

RIGHT Hug Me Kiddies were designed by Leon Rees of London who applied for a U.S. patent in 1912. The dolls were originally produced as a marketing incentive for magazines trying to get new children subscribers. The glass eyes swivel from side to side by means of a lever at the back of the head. This 1913 example has a worn face and is not wearing her original clothes and this, together with the fact that she is made of composition rather than the more desirable bisque, will reduce her value considerably.
Height: 14in (35.5cm)
Vaue: $250–400

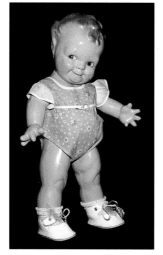

RIGHT The Cameo Doll Company produced a variety of Rose O'Neill's Scootles dolls in c.1925. The dolls have molded hair and jointed bodies and usually have the painted eyes of this doll; examples with sleeping eyes are more sought-after.
Height: 15¾in (40cm)
Value: $600–700

LEFT and ABOVE This 1935 Mary Hoyer doll has a knitted outfit from a pattern book called "Mary's Dollies," one of several released. Dolls with a set of outfits are highly prized.
Height: 14in (35.5cm)
Value: $350–450

LEFT EFFanBEE was the trademark of New York-based doll manufacturers Fleischaker & Baum, one of the top makers of composition dolls in the United States who registered its name in 1913. Many of the designs were based on characters from books or cartoons and included Anne Shirley from L. M. Montgomery's *Anne of Green Gables*. It first produced a Patsy doll in 1928 and followed this with others from the Patsy family including Wee Patsy, Patsy Joan, and Patsy Baby. Their slim bodies and pretty unjointed legs made them look particularly good in clothes, making them popular with children who could identify with this modern-looking girl doll. This c.1930 Patsy-Ann doll is marked on the back of her neck.
Height: 19in (48cm)
Value: $500–600

BELOW Although this is a poor-quality copy of the Patsy doll on the left, she still has some of the original's wistful charm. She is unmarked, there is damage to her nose and the paint is cracking behind her ears and on her head, and she is of considerably less value than the dolls of EFFanBEE.
Height: 9in (23.5cm)
Value: $25–50

LEFT and BELOW When a key is wound up in the side of this 1928 EFFanBEE Lovums "Hearbeat baby," its heart starts making a ticking sound!
Height: 18in (46cm)
Value: $500–800

RIGHT The Ideal Novelty and Toy Company of Brooklyn, New York City, was founded by Morris and Rose Michtom in 1903 to produce teddy bears and dolls. They first made a composition Shirley Temple doll in 1934 when the young actress was at the height of her fame in the United States, but continued to make the doll up until the 1970s in a range of materials and sizes. She was one of the most popular dolls ever produced as she represented the much-admired film star's world of escapism, laughter, and joy at a time of great deprivation in the United States. Although other manufacturers produced versions of the film star, those by Ideal are the most sought-after. This 1930s example, marked on the head and the body, is wearing her original pink net dress. Original clothes are particularly important and prices for rare outfits such as The Little Colonel or Captain January can be very high. The dress should be marked and ideally a large celluloid pin showing Shirley's face should still be attached to it.
Height: 17in (43cm)
Value: $600-900

LEFT and ABOVE In Canada the firm of Reliable Toys produced Shirley Temple dolls for Ideal. This 1930s example is wearing her original dress which is labeled. Reliable dolls vary greatly in quality, with some being very poor.
Height: 13in (33cm)
Value: $600-900

LEFT The Skookum trademark was registered by Mary McAboy for the Native American dolls produced for her by H.H. Tammen Co. from 1913 until the 1920s. The dolls represented various tribes and had their name printed on a label attached to the foot. The simple stick bodies were covered with painted woolen blankets and decorated with feathers and beads. This lady's dress is of dyed magenta doeskin and the cut leather strips have been used as lacing on her partner's costume. Their shoes are suede. Because the dolls were made in large numbers as souvenirs and many survive today, their prices have been slow to rise, but in recent years they have become quite collectible. This extraordinary pair are among the earliest examples and are beautifully made. Typically, their eyes are looking to the right; they rarely look to the left, and never straight ahead.
Height: 17/19in (43/48cm)
Value: $2,000-2,500 the pair

LEFT This 1930s Arranbee Nancy Lee has a slim adolescent body, which was a change from its earlier plump "Mama" dolls. Note the painted nails on a child doll.
Height: 21in (53cm)
Value: $300-400

RIGHT This topsy baby was made in the 1930s with the typical baby body and three tufts of wool hair on her head. However, she is a cheap copy of a popular doll made by a number of companies and is inaccurately modeled as a white baby painted black. Examples with their original clothes are more valuable.
Height: 9in (23.5cm)
Value: $50-75

LEFT Vogue Dolls Inc. of Medford, Massachusetts, was founded by Jennie Graves, who began by dressing imported dolls. The composition dolls have painted eyes and include Toddles, shown here. The dolls were all between 7in (18cm) and 8in (20cm) high and dressed in a wide variety of outfits.
Height: 8in (20cm)
Value: $200-350

FAR LEFT This 1940s Ginny doll is stamped with the name Priscilla on the sole of her right shoe and is appropriately dressed as a little Puritan girl. Ginny was first manufactured in the 1940s, but the name was not given until the 1950s. Ginny dolls were so popular that production continued in hard plastic from 1948 to 1962 (see p.148). They are still popular today because, apart from their appealing expressions, they are of a size that is easy to display in a glazed bookcase or glass cabinet.
Height: 7in (18cm)
Value: $250-350

Japanese Composition

Japan has a long history of making dolls for its girls' and boys' festivals; many were made to represent Samurai warriors and members of the court. The figures were handed down through generations and some survive from the 18th century. Most of those found in the West today date from the early 20th century.

ABOVE The body of this 19th-century Japanese doll (shown undressed, top) is of the type presented at the Great Exhibition of 1851 and subsequently copied for wax, bisque, china, and papier-mâché dolls made in France and Germany in the 1860s-1880s (see p.53 and p.60)—even down to the squeaker in the stomach. Notice the boy's anatomical detail. The

doll's body is incredibly light; the finish, called *gofun*, contains pulverized oyster shells and a binding agent. This "*mitsuore-ningyo*" is wearing his original beautifully decorated silk kimono.
Height: 15in (38cm)
Value: $1,000-1,800

ABOVE These two 1930s dolls were probably made for export. Called *Ichimatsu*, they are jointed to enable Japanese bowing or kneeling. Dressed in their original silk kimonos, they are in excellent condition and display the high quality of many *gofun*-finished Japanese dolls.
Height: 18in (46cm) each
Value: $900-1,200 the pair

Miscellaneous Composition

By the mid-1930s Europe was in a depression and bisque dolls, which were expensive to produce and easy to break, were widely replaced by composition headed examples, whose lower cost suited a large segment of the market. By the late 1930s quality declined, and dolls made during the Second World War were often quite ugly, as the emphasis was on producing goods for the war effort rather than luxury goods. Few serious collectors of antique dolls are interested in these late composition heads, but if you are lucky enough to find one of the better models in its original clothes, it will be interesting from a historical viewpoint because it fills the gap between the end of the bisque-headed era and the post-war boom in plastics.

BELOW Like so many composition dolls, this pretty little girl is not marked and it is not known who made her or where she is from. However, she is in excellent condition and is dressed in all her original clothes and as such would be an attractive addition to anyone's doll collection.
Height: 16in (40.5cm)
Value: $150-200

ABOVE This French version of the doll on the right is more realistically modeled, with molded curls and more detail in its features despite its smaller size. Although unmarked, it is thought to be French because of its likeness to a number of similar dolls found in that country. Dating to the 1940s, it has an inexpensive two-colored cloth body which originally would have been covered by its clothing.
Height: 9½in (24cm)
Value: $35-75

ABOVE The English firm of Pallitoy was set up by A. E Pallet in 1918. Pallet made dolls in cascelloid, a mixture of celluloid and composition which he hoped would not be flammable. The dolls, of which this one, made just before the Second World War, is an example, are marked on the head with "Plastex BNGM Flam, England." He has a cotton body and his amusing clothes are certainly contemporary and may be original.
Height: 13in (33cm)
Value: $45-85

ABOVE The English firm of Pedigree first made dolls in 1936 using by-products from the dolls' houses they were making. Although they produced a number of composition dolls, they are better known for the plastic dolls they made from the late 1940s (see p.151). This large 1930s composition girl is in excellent condition and is still wearing all her original clothes, including a hat and white boots.
Height: 20in (51cm)
Value: $50-150

Wax Dolls

Wax is a very versatile medium for doll-making as it melts under fairly low temperatures, can be poured into a mold, used as a coating, or be carved easily with a knife.

Munich was a center for wax-headed crèche figures made for religious use during the 18th century and probably earlier; and there are some magnificent, extremely rare English wax dolls made as playthings in the 18th century. These are usually modeled as fashionable women in elaborate clothes. Perhaps the first true wax baby dolls were the poured beeswax examples made in England at the turn of the 19th century. They have a yellow tint, sometimes wire-operated sleeping eyes, and carefully sewn robes and bonnets of the finest lawn.

The method of dipping a papier-mâché head into liquid wax appears to have begun very early in the 19th century in London yet it was not adopted as a method by the Germans until the 1860s, by which time English manufacturers had moved on to other ways of making dolls.

Although some of the famous English wax doll makers of the second half of the 19th century marked their dolls, many dolls today have lost their labels and are difficult to attribute.

Wax dolls were popular with collectors until the mid-20th century, when bisque characters took the lead, and they have never regained their popularity or comparable price levels.

LEFT (left to right) An English poured wax doll, c.1870; a German wax-over-composition headed doll, probaby Cuno and Otto Dressel, c.1880; and a German dipped bonnet head, c.1860.

RIGHT A Pierotti poured wax baby doll, c.1900.

Early Wax

Wax dolls made before 1850 are very rare today, because very few were made and only a tiny number have survived. They were very expensive to produce and were affordable only for the very rich. The earliest dolls were usually solid wax, with molded heads and cloth bodies. They were often dressed in very elaborate costumes and any that are still wearing their original clothes today will command a premium.

LEFT Early wax dolls often had painted hair. This small English child from c.1805 has the very short hair that was fashionable for both sexes at this time. Her eyes are tiny black glass beads like those of the other dolls on this page. She is hollow and very simply modeled—often the faces were far more elaborate. It is interesting to see how low the neck is cut on her original net dress.
Height: 7in (18cm)
Value: $600-1,000

BELOW Many early wax dolls were made in novelty form. These charming dancing piano dolls from c.1860 were placed on the piano to "dance" to the music—bristles underneath their skirts would move to the vibrations and cause them to jiggle about. These examples are a little too tall and tend to fall over, but they are extremely rare and desirable, particularly as they are still in their original, highly-decorated clothes.
Height: 3-4in (7.5-10cm)
Value: $500-1,000 the set

LEFT A common material for early wax dolls was beeswax, which was either melted down and poured into a mold or simply carved, giving the yellowy tint seen on the face of this figure, made c.1795. The fact that beeswax was expensive is reflected in the small size of his head. His hands are also made of wax; his body is cloth. Typically for early wax dolls, he has black bead eyes. He is dressed in a very elaborate Turkish costume of the type that was fashionable in the late 18th century.
Height: 10in (25.4cm)
Value: $1,000-2,000

English Dipped Wax

Dipped wax dolls were made by coating an already painted papier-mâché head in a layer of molten wax, which was a much less expensive alternative to the poured wax method (see pp.48-51). Made between c.1800 and 1860, these dipped wax dolls are more simply modeled than poured wax ones and may be of inferior quality but, because of their affordability, they are popular with collectors today.

ABOVE The crazing seen on the face of this c.1850 doll is very common among dipped wax dolls and is a result of the papier-mâché expanding more than the wax coating. When this happens, especially if the cracks are dirty, it will detract from the value. However, unless the face is totally bereft of wax the doll should not be re-dipped.
Height: 25in
(63.5cm)
Value: $250-400

BELOW Despite the fact that the faces of dipped wax dolls are often crudely modeled and are scantily painted, many of them still manage to have appealing expressions. This example, made in the 1860s, is of higher quality than many, free of crazing to the face, and with a beautifully arranged human hair wig, an elaborate dress, and a straw hat lined with lace.
Height: 24in (61cm)
Value: $1,000-1,500

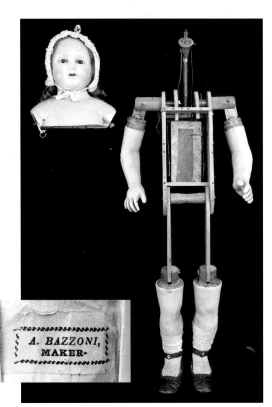

ABOVE Little is known about English doll manufacturer Bazzoni, except that he advertised himself in the 1860s as the only maker of talking dolls (they could say "Mama" and "Papa"). The dolls had wooden bodies and bellows in the chest that worked by moving the arms up and down. The sound passed through a brass pipe in the neck and out of the open mouth. This doll has a thicker layer of wax than most dipped wax dolls.
Height: 34in (86cm)
Value: $2,500-3,500

English Poured Wax

England's finest achievement in doll-making is arguably the poured wax-headed dolls made during the 19th century. For delicacy of modeling, realism in construction, charm, and quality of dressing, only the French bébés surpass them. Unfortunately, wax is very soft and many of the dolls have had their fine face paint and noses kissed away, been scratched or damaged, or even been melted down like the doll in Madame de Sevigny's novel *Les Malheurs de Sophy*!

Madame Augusta Montanari, Charles Marsh, the Pierottis, Charles Windsor, Herbert John Meech, John Edwards, Lucy Peck, and several other makers all produced very collectible dolls during the second half of the 19th century, and some continued to make them well into the 20th. The wax heads were fairly heavy as they were almost ¼in (5mm) thick and had inserted real hair. The head, arms, and legs were attached to thick cotton or linen bodies by sew holes made in the wax. Some dolls have metal or brass eyelets reinforcing the holes to take the force of the thread. Before being sold, dolls were usually dressed, predominantly as children in short lacy dresses, but Montanari clothed many of its dolls in elaborate silk outfits.

RIGHT When Queen Victoria and Prince Albert started to take their holidays at Balmoral in Scotland in the 1850s, Scottish things became very popular. Doll makers soon took advantage of this and started to produce dolls dressed in Highland costume. This good quality example from the 1880s is typical, wearing full outfit including tartan kilt and plaid.
Height: 22in (55cm)
Value: $1,200-2,000

RIGHT Domenico Pierotti came to London from Northern Italy c.1780 to establish what is now considered one of the highest-quality wax-modeling businesses. This early Pierotti, possibly from the 1860s, has short inserted real hair. Her pink wax arms are attached to her body with metal eyelets. Her value is increased by the fact that she is wearing her original whitework robe. Typical features include her soft facial details and well-defined fingers.
Height: 20in (51cm)
Value: $800–1,200

LEFT Augusta Montanari established her doll-making business in 1818. She worked from premises in London and, following her death in 1864 her son, Richard, took over. She dressed her dolls in highly elaborate clothes made in fine materials to her own design; her son's designs were simpler. Montanari dolls usually have the company name written in ink on part of the cloth body. This example was one of the award-winning dolls that appeared at the Great Exhibition in 1851. Typical Montanari features include the chubby arms, elaborate clothes, and down-turned mouth.
Height: 24in (61cm)
Value: $1,500–2,000

LEFT The down-turned mouth of this sad doll is like those found on Montanari dolls but because she is not marked she is classed as a "Montanari-type" doll. Her body is typically hand-stitched like that of a Montanari. Like some (but not all) Montanaris, she does not have metal eyelets attaching her arms to her body.
Height: 19in (48cm)
Value: $400–700

RIGHT Like many wax dolls, this example is not marked. The metal eyelets that hold the wax arms to the cloth body are clearly visible in this picture. Although this doll is not wearing her original clothes, the whitework baby's dress is contemporary with when she was made, in the mid-19th century. She is in very good condition.
Height: 20in (51cm)
Value: $600–900

RIGHT It is very unusual to find a wax doll in all its original clothes, especially when they are in such good condition as those on this example. Dressed as though she is going to a party, this 1850s doll is wearing a fine organdy dress painted in a delicate gold pattern and a blue under-dress trimmed with matching blue silk ribbons and pretty lace.
Height: 14in (35.5cm)
Value: $1,200–1,800

RIGHT Wax dolls modeled as boys, such as this sailor with his short inset hair, are much rarer than those dressed as girls. Poured wax dolls did not have jointed necks but this boy has been molded to glance slightly to his right. He is unmarked, but his clothes date him to c.1860.
Height: 16½in (42cm)
Value: $800–1,200

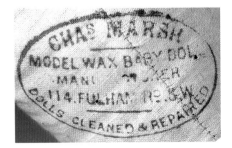

ABOVE This Charles Marsh stamp from the doll on the right clearly details his profession and the location of his workshop.

ABOVE Charles Marsh produced high-quality poured wax, composition, and wax-over-composition dolls between 1878 and 1895. He and his wife, Mary Anne Marsh, a doll repairer, operated from the same London address in Fulham Road and stamped their dolls on the body in black ink (see left). This doll has a beautiful serene expression. Made in the 1880s, she is still in excellent condition. The wax on her face has a slightly different, more yellow, coloring than that used for her pink arms and legs. Her value is increased by the fact that she is still wearing all her original clothes. The powder bloom on her face is still visible, giving her face a realistic soft flesh tone, and her hair, which would have been inserted individually strand by strand into the wax, is still in good condition.
Height: 22in (56cm)
Value: $1,000–1,500

PEDLAR DOLLS

This very high-quality wax pedlar doll is unusual because she is modeled as a pretty young girl rather than as the typical old woman. Her basket is heavily laden with wares and she is dressed in her original peasant-style costume and red cape. She was probably made by Henrietta Wade, an exceptional wax modeler who made figures of actors, Turks, ballet dancers, and other exotics in the 1840s. Most of her designs are so fragile that they can break at a touch, making them more like ornaments than playthings.
Height: 12in (30.5cm)
Value: $1,000–1,500

LEFT John Edwards was a prolific maker of wax dolls in the 1870s, based in Waterloo Road in London. Very few of his dolls were marked, so identifying them is difficult. This example is thought to have been made by him because the wax is typically pale and the details finely modeled. More a figurine than a plaything, he is sitting on his original plush cushion and is encased by a glass dome (not shown).
Height: 8in (20cm)
Value: $400–600

ABOVE Dolls with blue eyes became very popular after the birth of Queen Victoria's children. This example was made c.1850. The use of color underneath her bodice is particularly pretty and matches the silk bows on her sleeves and waist. She also has her own nightgown and a muff, which is still with its original box.
Height: 22in (55cm)
Value: $1,000–1,500

German Wax

German manufacturers used two different methods to make wax dolls. The first copied the English method, where light, molded heads of papier-mâché were painted and then dipped in a very thin coating of wax to give a softer more flesh-like finish. The bodies were made of muslin, usually fitted with a squeaker, and had brightly-painted wooden limbs. The second method produced a higher-quality doll. The wax was poured into a mold, allowed to solidify until less than ⅛in (2mm) thick and then poured out. A liquid pink plaster was then poured on to reinforce the wax and give a flesh tone to the head before being poured out again. Eyes were inserted, sometimes of the sleeping type, and the features were painted on. Unfortunately, with atmospheric changes the plaster/composition often expands and the wax can crack. The bodies are again of stuffed cotton, but the arms and legs are usually of well-modeled composition with a wax coating. The molded boots or shoes on the feet help to date the dolls.

LEFT Pumpkin-heads, made in Germany from c.1860, were so-called because their large hollow heads, molded and dipped in wax, resembled pumpkins. This little lady pumpkin-head is missing her skirt (not shown), but fortunately, because her feathered hat is molded as part of her head, she has managed to keep it on: small wisps of hair are glued under the brim.
Height: 12in (30.5cm)
Value: $150-250

RIGHT Small nails behind the ears of this pumpkin-head suggest she may at one time have worn a wig. Like most German dipped dolls, this doll's clothes were not made to be changed and the fact that she is still wearing her original, elaborately decorated silk dress and that it is still in good condition will increase her value.
Height: 15in (38cm)
Value: $200-300

ABOVE This 1860s Taufling doll is of a type based on Japanese dolls (p.42)—the thin dipped papier-mâché head even has Japanese-style tufts of hair painted at the nape and behind each ear. The weighted sleeping eyes are the only feature it does not share with its Japanese prototype.
Height: 12in (30.5cm)
Value: $400-600

RIGHT Wax-over-composition dolls were much more realistically modeled than the earlier dipped wax examples, and indicated a degree of skill in doll-making that was to come into its own with bisque dolls. This pretty girl, made in the 1880s, is still in excellent condition, showing no wear to her face or clothes. Because these dolls were made in large quantities and generally from inexpensive materials, they tend to remain affordable today. Only exceptional examples, like the doll on page 7 will command a premium.
Height: 19in (48cm)
Value: $300-500

CHRISTMAS TIME!
Prince Albert is said to have introduced the decorated Christmas tree into Britain at the end of the 19th century. This led to large quantities of inexpensive Christmas tree fairies, as the traditional European angel was not considered suitable for Protestant England. Because the fairies were brought out only one year, they tend to be in good condition, and this example, usually kept under a glass dome, is no exception. Her muslin dress, tinsel, wings, wand, and hair decoration are all original and her blonde mohair wig is as good as new. Her body is of cheap cotton.
Height: 14in (35cm)
Value: $250-500

ABOVE These two unusual pumpkin-head Christmas tree dolls have cheap cotton bodies and painted wooden arms and legs. Their original fancy dresses decorated with gold paper are still in excellent condition. Their hats have metal rings attached for hanging them on the tree.
Height: 12in (30cm) each
Value: $300-500 the pair

CHINA DOLLS

It always seems surprising in view of their fragile nature that so many china-headed dolls have survived, and it is a tribute to the good behavior of Victorian children and perhaps to the vigilance of their parents and nurses that we can enjoy them today. Some china dolls' heads were made in France and Denmark, but the major source was Germany, where many small firms in the Sonneberg area produced high-quality examples from the 1840s to 1870s, although production continued to the end of the century.

The heads vary considerably in quality, generally getting poorer towards the end of the century. The faces are normally modeled as women and have painted eyes, although some early French dolls by Madame Rohmer and Madame Huret sometimes have inset glass eyes. When buying lady dolls, look for unusual hairstyles or hair colors, hair ornaments, molded collars, necklaces, or bodices. Dolls with fine painting and a pink hue are greatly sought-after, as are those with brush strokes round the temples indicating brushed-back hair.

Very few china heads are marked, but of those makers who did mark their dolls, the most important are Jacob Petit of Paris, the Royal Copenhagen Factory, and the Royal Porcelain Factory in Berlin.

LEFT (left to right) A German shoulder head, 1880s, holding a German doll's house doll, c.1900; an interesting German china baby with domed bald head, c.1870; and a German shoulder head of c.1865.

RIGHT A German domed china headed doll from c.1870.

China Heads

Most china heads that survive today date from the 19th century. Jacob Petit in Paris started making heads c.1830, while the Royal Porcelain Factory in Berlin, and possibly Meissen, Copenhagen, and other German factories were in production from the 1840s. Dating is only possible by the hairstyle and sometimes the quality of the painting and flesh tone, but even this is not a sure-fire method as molds were often used over an extended period. During the 1850s and 1860s many major German and French firms made china heads, but after the introduction of bisque, the popularity of glazed china declined and by the 1890s most china heads were of poor quality.

LEFT The tightly coiled bun suggests this doll is one of the earliest china heads, probably made in the 1840s. She is particularly desirable because of the brown color of her hair and the elaborate molded flowers on either side of her head. Although she is a rare doll, she is found in at least two sizes, of which the larger is often more beautifully detailed. This smaller example has a slight blemish in the glaze which will detract from her value. Her simply constructed body is of kid leather. Her petticoat is contemporary with the date she was made, but her apron is from the 1860s.
Height: 15in (38cm)
Value: $3,400-4,500

ABOVE *Autoperipatetikos*, or clockwork walking dolls, are a specialized collectible. The walking design was patented in the United States in 1862 and dolls were made with many different heads and in a variety of materials. This German china-headed example sports a lovely hairstyle that was fashionable among women in the 1860s. Originally, she would have been wearing an elaborate silk dress, but sadly this must have rotted with age, and she is now wearing an inferior replacement.
Height: 10in (25.4cm)
Value: $600-1,200

LEFT Contrasting this little scrap of a doll from the 1840s with the one next to her shows the difference in quality among china dolls. There is only a minimal attempt at a hairstyle, just whirls of black paint. The face is sparsely and unevenly painted, the eyebrows in particular. She has the most basic of kid bodies, and despite her petticoats, would look more at home dressed as a man!
Height: 10in (25.4cm)
Value: $200-350

LEFT The molded black curls of this charming 1850s pink-tinted boy are found on many German china heads made between the 1850s and 1890s, with only slight differences in the parting, ringlets, and hairline. China dolls with this pinkish hue are particularly sought-after; most china-headed dolls have only patches of rouge on their cheeks. This one's hairstyle is actually that of a woman, but the man's clothes, contemporary with the time he was made, suit him well! Men are much rarer than women, and any in the excellent condition of this example will command a solid price, even when it's only the "clothes that make the man."
Height: 9in (23.5cm)
Value: $400-700

ABOVE China dolls with the brown eyes of this pink-toned woman are rare and sought-after. Her simple, domed hairstyle, which dates her to the 1850s, is known in the United States as the "covered wagon" as it resembles the hairstyle most commonly worn by the brave women who set off for the unknown in the West, suffering privation and hardship to find a new life for themselves here. Her china hands are unusual because they are cupped. Her dress is home-made, but the use of checked and plain colored silk is pleasing, especially the piping around the neck and bodice.
Height: 20in (51cm)
Value: $800-1,200

HAIRSTYLES

Looking at the hairstyles of china dolls can indicate when the dolls were made, while the level of detail reflects the quality: generally, simpler modeling indicates a doll of lesser quality. China heads with particularly elaborate hairstyles or those that have decorations, such as china flowers or hairbands, are also more difficult to find and thus more highly collectible.

1840s

1850s

1850s

1880s

1880s

1880s-90s

RIGHT The strongly defined center parting in the hairstyle of this charming china head doll suggests she was made in the late 1850s. The rather stiff wooden arms are not original and the dress is a copy of a design fashionable in the 1840s, but she is still a desirable doll.
Height: 19in (48cm)
Value: $450-700

LEFT The delicate facial molding, the bright rouged cheeks, and swept back hair of this c.1870 china head are all indications of high quality. She has a kid body and china arms which are visible beneath her lacy sleeves.
Height: 15in (38cm)
Value: $1,500

COLLECTOR'S TIPS

Certain factors should be taken into consideration when buying a china-headed doll.

Quality
Look for high-quality modeling with careful painting, pink tinting, and no blemishes or chips in the china. Take care when handling dolls as the china feet can knock together. Also, as molds were used many times over, a doll early out of the mold will have sharper detail than one from a well-used mold.

Hairstyles
The more elaborate hairstyles are the most sought-after, with any additional decoration, such as hairbands or bows, adding value.

Clothes
Dolls wearing their original clothes are highly desirable and, being rare, command a premium. If not original, the clothes should suit the style and period of the doll.

RIGHT Although china heads usually have black hair, some later examples, such as this girl from the 1880s, had blond hair. This doll has the added details of a blue band holding back her curls and painted blue garters above her boots, both of which are attractive features.
Height: 13¼in (34cm)
Value: $300–500

RIGHT Some dolls, like this one, with their hair curled low onto their forehead, are known as "lowbrows" after their hairstyle, which dates this doll to the 1890s, when the look was fashionable (the doll below sports a similar style). They continued to be made into the early 20th century and are found more often than earlier dolls. These later dolls tend to be of poorer quality than earlier ones—note the uneven painting on this girl's boots—and consequently are less sought-after by collectors.
Height: 11in (28cm)
Value: $50–125

RIGHT Solid china standing dolls became known as Frozen Charlies or Charlottes after an American poem about a girl called Charlotte who was too vain to wear a coat over her pretty clothes when she set out for a dance one bitterly cold evening and arrived there frozen to death. This little boy has a nicely painted face with a pink flesh tone. The dolls are also called bathing dolls because their hollow, highly-glazed bodies enable them to float in a bath. They were made in a variety of sizes from 1 inch (2.5cm) to approximately 16 inches (40cm) high. In England, the smallest ones were "pudding dolls," baked in the Christmas pudding; when found in a slice it signified that the recipient was assured of having a baby the following year.
Height: 10½in (26.6cm)
Value: $200-350

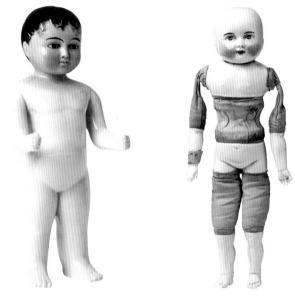

LEFT and ABOVE RIGHT The construction of this china-headed baby is copied from the Japanese dolls exhibited at the Great Exhibition in 1851. It is almost identical, down to a squeaker in the body and a turning head, but without the floating hands and feet and missing the male anatomical detail, which was considered inappropriate for Western children. Many other manufacturers copied this construction, including Jules Nicolas Steiner and a number of German makers, who sometimes dipped the heads in thin wax to provide a coating (see p.53). This example has a damaged arm, affecting its value.
Height: 12in (30.5cm)
Value: $600-900

EARLY CHINAS

France was one of the first countries to make china-headed dolls. Jacob Petit made lovely lady dolls with molded hair arranged in plaits circling the ears and head. Some of Madame Rohmer's and Madame Huret's early dolls had china heads, many of which look more child-like and chubby-faced than the later fashionable French lady dolls (see pp.66-7). French chinas are very rare because they were made in very small quantities and for only a short period, between 1840 and 1860. Prices are therefore higher than for their German counterparts.

LEFT The hairstyle of this china head, coiled in a braid around the sides of the head and with a chignon of hair at the nape of the neck, dates her to around the 1860s. Sadly, she is rather faded, which will detract from her value.
Head height: 5¼in (13cm)
Value: $400-600

LEFT There is some question as to where these beautiful flesh-toned heads were made but they are probably English. Found either as young adults or as a well-fed child, their faces are particularly realistic. Rare for china dolls, the legs (not shown), are modeled without shoes or boots. The heads have six holes around the base of the shoulders for attaching it to the body.
Height: 20in (51cm)
Value: $2,500-4,000

LEFT This 1840s' china head is a lovely example of Jacob Petit's work. She has a stuffed kid body with individually stitched fingers and is wearing a contemporary dress of white muslin, original underclothes, and leather slippers. She has a black underglaze mark on the front of her chest which reads "Par Brevet," meaning that the design was patented.
Height: 15½in (40cm)
Value: $2,500-4,000

ABOVE This chubby-cheeked German lady is typical of the more ordinary china heads made in the late 1880s. Her hair is curled simply around her face, her mouth is small, and her cheeks are deeply red. The original stuffed cotton body has china limbs, with hands outspread, and she is wearing molded black heeled boots. It is likely that her silk dress is later and home-made.
Height: 14in (35.5cm)
Value: $175-250

Bisque Dolls

It wasn't until the 1860s that developments in industrial techniques made it financially viable to produce dolls' heads in a porcelain known as bisque. This consisted of a white kaolin paste base which was fired, painted a flesh tone, then fired again. Left unglazed, bisque heads have a more natural looking matte finish than the earlier high-glazed china heads.

By the 1860s many French firms were making bisque heads with painted features and an open dome for a wig. Quality peaked in Paris in the 1870s and 80s, when bisque socket heads were designed with such artistry and painted so delicately that they reproduced the ideal vision of a Victorian child.

The Germans also made bisque heads, often with molded hairstyles. More efficient than the small French firms, they were soon supplying Europe and America, and by the end of the 1890s, their impact was so great that the French banded together to form a single society, SFBJ, producing dolls in far greater numbers, but of a much lesser quality than earlier.

Bisque was used for dolls' heads until the Second World War, although toward the end of the period on less expensive dolls the heads were sometimes fired white and then spray-painted.

LEFT (left to right) A French lady doll with Gaultier head and jointed Gesland body, 1870s; a German shoulder head in original clothes, 1860s, holding an all-bisque dolls' house doll, c.1920; an Armand Marseille doll, mold 1894, in original clothes, c.1900.

RIGHT
A German child doll with voice box and pull-string mechanism.

FRENCH LADY DOLLS

The beautiful china and bisque head dolls with slim bodies, made in Paris from the 1860s to the early 20th century, have been given many names, including Parisiennes, Fashion dolls, French fashions, and Fashionable dolls. A French magazine devoted to the promotion of these dolls, *La Poupée Modèle,* published fashion plates, instructions, and paper patterns for making the dolls' clothes and furniture, as well as homilies on good behavior, which are useful when trying to date the dolls today.

French lady dolls are often difficult to attribute. Many are not marked, and sometimes the label or stamp is of the store where they were sold rather than the maker. In most cases the heads and bodies were made by different people. Even so, there are distinguishing features of, for example, an early Bru or Rohmer which help attribute them to their maker.

Dolls made before 1860 are usually of glazed china with painted features. Later developments include set-in glass eyes, swivel neck articulation, and the use of unglazed bisque. Although sometimes dressed as children or babies, they reached the height of expression as ladies dressed in the fashionable costumes of the day, which they now enchantingly record.

Bodies

The bodies of French lady dolls are always of a slim, adult form, with the limbs in good proportion to the body and head. Most of the bodies are of stuffed kid, but variations include wood, kid applied over wood, leather, metal, and gutta percha; some have bisque or china arms.

This Huret body is of rare jointed gutta percha, once light and easy to mold but now extremely brittle.

A Rohmer body with heavy bisque arms, kid over wood upper arms, joints at the shoulder, and pivot knee joints.

A kid over wood Rohmer body but with tongue and groove joints and a thinner, lower waistline, c.1870.

A simple Rohmer body with basic jointing of simple gussets at the bottom and knee and slack kid at the shoulder.

A Bru jointed turned wood body. These bodies allow the greatest movement and are some of the most desirable.

A Gaultier head with a metal Gesland jointed body covered in stockinette; the hands and feet are bisque, c.1875.

The most common lady body, probably the least expensive, of gusseted kid with separate fingers often individually wired.

An early 1880s Bru body showing how the jointed wooden body of the lady doll has been adapted to suit a young child.

A late lady Huret doll, c.1910, with a jointed wood body, molded breasts, and a very slim waist.

Maison Huret

Madame Calixte Huret was one of the most important early Par doll-makers. Her dolls from the 1850s and early 1860s had cl shoulder heads, often with painted eyes and with no ear pierci The bisque shoulder heads were similar in modeling, probably tak from the same molds. It is likely that her 1861 patent was the ear liest given for a socket head. Certainly she was very innovative using various bodies and jointing mechanisms. She is particularl noted for her fine dolls' clothes which are stamped with "Huret' on the inside waistband. Her house provided everything a doll could want, including high-quality furniture with seats uphol-stered in silk, and tassels falling from the sides of tables.

LEFT This lovely c.1863 doll has almost flat ears, pierced into the head, which are an indication of Madame Huret's early dolls. She still has her store label and box from la Petite Amazone from Maison Delacroix in Paris, but typically no maker's mark as most smart stores wanted to mark dolls themselves. She may possibly have been a special order as she has an extensive wardrobe including accessories. She has the typical swivel head of Huret dolls, on a bisque shoulder plate, a kid over wood body, jointed at the shoulders, elbows, hips, and knees. Her chunky arms are of pale bisque and she has the typical indented knuckles of Huret dolls.
Height: 18in (46cm)
Value: $8,000-12,000

ABOVE Madame Huret used many types of bodies for her dolls; those with bisque arms are desirable. This late 1850s body is of gusseted kid over wood and her arms are modeled from above the elbow.
Height: 15in (38cm)
Value: $3,500-5,500

RIGHT The doll on the left has an unusual flange neck joint. Her upper arms and knees are kid over wood, but her arms from the elbow are of finely modeled bisque. She is wearing her original silk dress with military styling. The only mark she has is the number 4, and sadly her store label on her chest has been torn off, but she may have been made by Madame Rohmer. Her companion is a fabulous Huret doll with a very rare gutta percha body (see p.65) which was only used between the 1850s and 1860s, most prominently by Huret.
Height: 17in (43cm) each
Value: left $3,000-4,000; right $9,000-15,000

Madame Rohmer

Madame Marie Antoinette Léontine Rohmer is known to have made dolls between 1857 and 1880, although it is probable that she was already well-established as a doll-maker when she applied for her first patent in 1857 for dolls with articulated kid bodies and arms of gutta percha or rubber.

She was obviously proud of her work and the quality of her dolls, as so many of her dolls are marked with her oval stamp on the body. She patented several designs, including a kid or wood ball and socket joint at the knee, strings coming from holes in the body to tie the legs in a sitting position, and china legs modeled with bare feet, an idea copied by Gesland.

Perhaps one of the most distinguishing features of her dolls are the well-modeled and heavy bisque or china arms with the suggestion of a knuckle and the hand cupped as if it is about to hold something. Her dolls, particularly marked examples, are sought after by experienced collectors. Those with rare body types and/or their original clothes are highly desirable.

ABOVE The early Rohmer dolls of the late 1850s/early 1860s were shoulder heads rather than swivel heads. This china example has deep inset blue eyes, single color lip painting, and long, pale eyebrows achieved by making a number of fine brush strokes. Her body is of simple kid leather, and she is wearing a rather tattered silk dress, which is much too large for her.
Height: 15in (38cm)
Value: $2,000–3,000

LEFT This Rohmer doll is particularly interesting because the face is round and full-cheeked with an innocent childlike expression and she is dressed as a baby, wearing her original whitework robe. Many early Rohmer dolls—this one was made in the early 1860s—were dressed as children with short skirts. The doll has the china head and painted eyes of early dolls, with a heavy black line above the eye and a lighter eyebrow. This type of neck is known as a flange neck because the head and shoulder pieces are flat and swivel over each other like a grindstone. The unruly sheepskin wig is a typical feature of Rohmer's dolls. The lovely china arms are joined to a wood upper arm which has a hinge and tenon joint at the shoulder. An identical doll was made in bisque.
Height: 21in (53cm)
Value: $6,000–9,000

ABOVE Later Rohmer dolls had the inset glass eyes seen on this c.1865 example, which give the doll a more alive appearance and make her more appealing to some collectors. She has a flange neck and bisque arms which are modeled to make her particularly appealing.
Height: 16in (41cm)
Value: $3,000–4,500

François Gaultier

From 1860 to 1899 François Gaultier probably made more bisque dolls' heads and parts than any other porcelain factory in and around Paris. The firm (called Gaultier from 1875) sold its heads to other makers and its heads appear on a variety of bodies and clockwork toys by many of the top French toy makers. Automata by Vichy and some of the most beautifully dressed lady dolls with store-stamped bodies have Gaultier heads. Many of the kid-bodied lady dolls have FG heads which may be marked with the initials and size number on the shoulders. Gesland also attached Gaultier heads to its bodies on both lady and child dolls. Gaultier's quality is varied, from the superb ladies to the inexpensive souvenir dolls, often with poor-quality FG heads.

BELOW This c.1860 lady doll in original dress is an example of the lesser quality heads that Gaultier produced. She has simply-painted features and an unjointed kid body with no finger definition.
Height: 12in (30.5cm)
Value: $400–500

LEFT This juxtaposition of an early and a late lady doll offers an interesting comparison. The later lady on the left has a slightly surprised expression, possibly caused by the eye-brows, which are raised in astonishment. Her heavy eye-brows, usually found on later dolls, date her to the 1890s. She has a rigid kid body with no gussets, and the typical separately stitched and wired fingers. She still has her origi-nal underclothes but her dress and coat have been re-made. Her early companion on the right has softer eyebrows and mouth painting. Other early features are her gusseted body, longer mouth, and small eyes, which although still bulbous, are less piercing. Gaultier made heads for Jumeau before he set up his own business and this may be an example.
Height: left 18½in (47cm); right 18in (46cm)
Value: left $1,400–1,800; right $2,500–3,500

RIGHT Gesland jointed bodies consisting of a metal armature covered in kapok and stockinette, often have Gaultier heads with bisque hands and legs jointed at the wrist and knee, as in the example here.
Height: 15in (38cm)
Value: $2,000-3,000

FAR RIGHT The human hair wig of this c.1870 doll is likely to be a replacement for an original one of mohair. She has the typical gusseted kid-leather body with separately stitched fingers and toes and is wearing her original dress.
Height: 20in (51cm)
Value: $2,000-2,800

FAR LEFT Some later 1890s adult dolls with Gaultier heads were not dressed as fashionable women. This example, wearing her original children's nurse's clothes, including a long warm wool cape and elaborate hat, looks like she is just about to push the perambulator out in the park!
Height: 18in (46cm)
Value: $2,000-2,800

LEFT The original red mohair wig of this size 4 Gaultier-headed doll is very unusual. Her face is beautifully painted and she is wearing a delightfully simple muslin summer bodice and skirt. Her high-heeled boots are stamped "FG" on the heel.
Height: 17½in (45cm)
Value: $1,500-2,500

Jumeau

The firm of Jumeau was set up in 1842 by Pierre Jumeau to produce dolls with kid leather bodies dressed in the fine fashions of the day and with heads supplied by other makers; the earliest examples are thought to have been made of papier-mâché and supplied from Sonneberg. By the 1870s Jumeau was using all-bisque French heads but they are often unmarked and so are difficult to attribute today. Occasionally "Jumeau" is found stamped in blue on the lower back of a kid-bodied doll.

LEFT and ABOVE Although this large fashionable doll is not marked, there are several features which identify her as a Jumeau, including the shaded lids Jumeau also used for its bébés (see pp.78-81). Other typical characteristics include:
• swivel neck on a bisque shoulder plate
• gusseted kid body with separate fingers and toes
• applied ears
• bulbous eyes
The close-up of the doll's face clearly shows the characteristic blue spiral glass eyes, sometimes referred to as paperweight eyes, of Jumeau dolls. Another feature that can be seen here are the applied ears which are pierced into the lobe; on earlier examples they are pierced into the head.
Height: 26in (66cm)
Value: $4,500-5,500

ABOVE Jumeau made dolls in many sizes. This example is only 12in (30.5cm) high but still displays all the quality of the larger dolls, including prominent blue eyes, finely stitched gusseted kid body, and swivel neck. The fact that she is wearing her original dress will add to her value.
Height: 12in (30.5cm)
Value: $2,000-2,800

Bru

Léon Casimir Bru founded the firm of Bru Jeune et Cie in 1866 and until 1883 made lady dolls with heads supplied by other manufacturers. Bru heads are found on a variety of bodies, including all kid, kid with bisque or jointed wooden arms, and all wood articulated bodies. The dolls are usually marked with the firm's name or initials, or with a size letter between A and L. Brus are among the most sought-after and collectible dolls today and command some of the highest prices at auction.

ABOVE Although the modeling of this superb head is similar to that of the doll below left, the painting of the facial details is very different. Dolls such as this, with the wooden jointed body introduced by Bru in 1871, are very desirable as they can be moved into many positions. Height: 18in (46cm) Value: $4,500-7,000

ABOVE The modeling of this Bru is not as fine as on some dolls, but she has exceptional hands. She is wearing her original 1880s clothes which were tighter and straighter than earlier, and with fussy gatherings and pleats from neck to hem. They are not as flattering, the materials were heavier, and the colors not as fresh as they had been in the 1860s and 1870s. Height: 20in (51cm) Value: $3,500-4,500

ABOVE In 1873 Bru registered this smiling doll with a swivel head on a bisque shoulder plate. She has a cloth body, kid arms, and separately-stitched fingers. To find her in her original dress is rare and desirable even though her cloth body suggests she was one of Bru's less expensive dolls. Height: 11in (28cm) Value: $3,000-4,000

ABOVE This Bru marked "B" has the classic Bru kid body with bisque arms, and hands that are exquisitely modeled in a curved position with ladylike grace. The original costume is magnificent and perfectly preserved, greatly increasing her value. Her face has particularly high cheek coloring and her long, delicately curled smiling mouth has an attractive accentuated cupid's bow on the upper lip. Height: 12in (30.5cm) Value: $4,000-6,000

Other French Lady Dolls

French lady dolls differed enormously in price and quality when they were made in the late 1860s to 1880s; the dolls from the larger firms often varied the most. French doll-makers were usually assemblers rather than manufacturers, buying fine-quality bisque heads from small specialist porcelain plants or from François Gaultier who when his wife died left a long list of debtors that included many top firms. All the major Paris doll stores, including Madame Lavalée-Peronne, Simonne, and Au Paradis des Enfants, put their own stamp or label on dolls they bought to sell. They dressed the dolls to their tastes, or sold the clothing off the rack to the retail buyer. If the label or stamp on a doll also has an address on it, it was probably attached by a retail outfit advertising its products. Dolls with retail labels are just as important as those with makers' marks: many of them are of exceptional quality and have magnificent wardrobes.

RIGHT E. Barrois sold dolls' heads in Paris between 1858 and 1894 and it is likely that this doll marked "E Deposé I B" was made by him in the 1860s. It has deep cobalt blue eyes with pale brows, a long mouth painted in two shades of pink, pierced ears, and a swivel neck. Her gusseted kid body has separately sewn fingers and she is wearing all her magnificent original clothes. The turquoise of her earring was a fashionable color for jewelry made for dolls in Paris at this time.
Height: 13½in (34cm)
Value: $2,500-3,500

LEFT The pink cheeks of this large lady doll suggest she is slightly later, dating from c.1870. She displays all the typical features of fashionables, but her hair arranged in ringlets is a rather childish style for the time. She is wearing a contemporary blue silk taffeta dress with cut picot edging and a rosette at her waist that was often found on children's dresses.
Height: 22½in (57cm)
Value: $2,500-3,000

LEFT The unusual face of this doll, with its very high arched eyebrows, protruding philtrum, and small pouting mouth, has not yet been attributed to a maker and the doll bears no mark. It is likely she was made in the 1870s, although her clothes are later. She has a real hair wig and a gusseted kid leather body with separately stitched fingers and toes.
Height: 21in (53cm)
Value: $2,000-3,000

ABOVE This fashionable doll from the late 1860s/early 1870s is impressed "B7S" on her shoulder plate. It is considered to be the mark of Blampoix Senior and appears regularly on heads, the number representing the size. Dolls stamped "BS" are known to have been marketed by Alphonse Giroux of 43 Boulevard des Capucines, one of the major 19th century Paris doll dealers.
Height: 23in (58.5cm)
Value: $2,800-3,800

RIGHT The solid appearance of this lady reflects the fact that she is a less expensive lady doll. However, the fact that she is accompanied by an extra dress in the fashion of the 1860s makes her attractive.
Height: 13in (33cm)
Value: $1,500-2,000

FRENCH BÉBÉS

It is not certain which French doll maker first introduced a child-like doll. Some of the early Huret and Rohmer heads are certainly not very ladylike, with their plump cheeks and round faces, and Steiner produced an early child doll that was similar in construction to the Japanese composition headed dolls shown at the International Exhibition in London in 1851.

By the end of the 1870s many French makers, including Léon Casimir Bru and Émile Jumeau were selling child dolls which have been known as bébés ever since, to distinguish them from German child dolls.

The beautiful creations of the French firms during the 1880s probably represent the peak of doll-making. They were high-quality, luxury items with fashionable clothes of expensive materials, and the artistry of the modeling and skill in the molding and painting, as well as the body construction, make them one of the most admired areas of doll-collecting today.

There is a surprising number of makers, each with its individual style. Price depends on rarity but also beauty, so some Bru and Jumeau dolls that are in greater supply can command higher prices than more elusive dolls that may be less attractive. Also, do not judge by maker alone; look for fine bisque, good painting, and original clothes. Dolls that are both rare and beautiful such as those made by Halopeau and Thuillier command the highest prices, and if you are a beginner considering the purchase of an expensive bébé, you should seek professional advice.

Bru

Léon Casimir Bru established the firm of Bru Jeune in 1866 and by the end of the 1870s was producing a variety of fine and often innovative bébés which today are the prize of many a collection. In business during the same period as the Maison Jumeau, and with a factory alongside it in Montreuil-sous-Bois, the two doll-makers were rivals for the high end of the doll market. However, because Bru made considerably fewer dolls than Jumeau, his bébés tend to be rarer and more sought-after today. In 1899 Bru became a member of the SFBJ which continued to produce dolls from the Bru molds and marked with the Bru name until the middle of the 20th century. However, these are of inferior quality and bear little resemblance to the earlier dolls.

LEFT Bru's first bébé, the Bru Breveté, portrays a young child with a very innocent look. This 1870s example is typical, with its kid body and pressed bisque head with a cork pate. Like the early lady dolls, the Breveté has ears pierced into its head. The beautifully modeled bisque hands look strangely out of place on this fat-cheeked and fat-bodied toddler, but it is interesting to see elements that developed into one of the most beautiful range of dolls ever produced. The sizing on these dolls indicates reductions of the mold from size 0; the smallest is 6/0 (the sixth reduction) at 9½in (24cm). This example is 4/0, which is 11½in (29cm). These early dolls were marked only with the size and not with the maker.
Height: 11½in (29cm)
Value: $8,000-12,000

RIGHT This 1886 child doll is a particularly fine example of a Bru bébé, in perfect condition including her clothes. Her fetching straw hat is lined with deep red velvet to match her lovely dress. Note how the arm length is now in proportion to the body and the face is modeled as a slightly older child than the Breveté. Her lower legs are now of wood and she is jointed at the shoulder, hip, and knee.
Height: 15in (38cm)
Value: $18,000-28,000

LEFT This c.1880s bébé is known as a Circle and Dot because it has the mark of a circle with a dot inside it on the back of its head. The mouth is molded slightly open, showing a row of painted teeth between the lips. The bisque shoulder plate has a molded breast and the body is of gusseted kid, with the typically finely-molded bisque hands. She is wearing a lovely original silk dress edged with a contrasting color and is carrying her straw hat lined with plum silk.
Height: 20½in (52cm)
Value: $16,000-25,000

LEFT One of Bru's most innovative designs is this bébé Gourmand or eating doll. She has a tube running from her mouth to the sole of her bisque foot. The shoe, missing on this doll, also has a flap in the sole to allow the food out!
Height: 20in (50cm)
Value: $25,000-30,000

ABOVE In the 1880s, after the introduction of the Breveté, Bru patented this Bru Jne, with a swivel neck, bisque shoulder plate, molded young girls' breasts, and kid body. She has delicately molded hands of pale tinted bisque, upper arms of kid over wood, and lower legs of carved and painted wood. There is a suggestion of a tongue and she has heavily shaded eyelids. The seams of the original wig are visible but this is far preferable to a replacement. She is probably too big and heavy for a young girl to handle.
Height: 29in (74cm)
Value: $18,000-28,000

DOLL NAME	DATE	CHARACTERISTICS
Bru Brévéte	1870s	Gusseted kid body, bisque arms, skin wig.
Circle and Dot	1870s and early 80s	Early kid body, molded breasts. Mark of a circle surrounding a dot.
Bru Jne	1880s	Molded breastplate with nipples, bisque arms and wooden (or sometimes kid) legs.
Bébé Teteur	1880 through SFBJ period	Open mouth to accommodate a bottle.
Bébé Gourmand	1881	Open mouth, body tube for pellets.

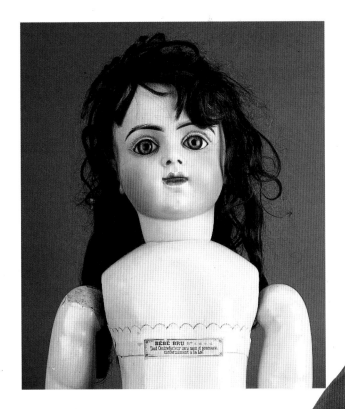

ABOVE In the 1890s Bru was taken over by the firm of Paul Girard, which made less expensive dolls with "Bru Jne R" impressed on the back of the head. This example has the typical wood and composition body with the characteristic serrated kid band around the chest bearing the Bru paper label. She is fitted with a voice box mechanism operated by a pull string. Her dark, long eyebrows reflect the fashion of the time, and her eyelashes seem to grow mainly from the fold of the eye lid.
Height: 30in (76.5cm)
Value: $9,000–15,000

RIGHT Some of Bru's later bébés of the 1880s had the straight-wrist wood and composition jointed body of this lovely matador. His expression, almost smiling and delicately painted, is superb and yet strangely unheroic against his most unusual original costume. It is possible this doll was made for the Spanish market as the dark eyes and mohair wig go well with the red and blue satin Spanish costume. The head is the standard Bru head, so his pierced ears have been left unadorned. He is impressed "Bru Jne 8" and has "Bru Jne Paris" on the sole of one shoe. This doll in such an unusual outfit would please the most exacting collector.
Height: 18½in (47cm)
Value: $14,000–18,000

Jumeau

Jumeau is perhaps the best-known of all the French doll houses. Both Pierre François and Émile Jumeau produced high-quality dolls, but it was Émile who understood the power of advertising, making Jumeau into the largest doll company in France with its own porcelain factory for heads at Montreuil-sous-Bois. Their output of bébés was phenomenal, and although they turn up regularly, prices, even for late dolls, remain high. The early bébés command a premium, especially those of the late 1870s and early 1880s, with their shaded eyelids and almond-shaped eyes. The EJ "A" mold and "long faces" are also highly desirable, as are those with bodies with eight separate ball joints and straight wrists. When choosing a Jumeau doll, look for quality of paintwork and the color of the bisque. The earlier pressed bisque heads with their soft expressions are always preferable to the later ones.

ABOVE So-called portrait Jumeaus were introduced in 1877. This example has the characteristic almond-shaped eyes with shaded lids, and irises with a simple darker striation encircled by a dark blue rim. She is of pale pressed bisque and her lightweight papier-mâché body has the desirable eight separate balls at the joints and fixed wrists (shown at the top of the next page).
Height: 16in (40.5cm)
Value: $6,000–9,000

RIGHT This lovely Émile Jumeau bébé from c.1880, with her soft coloring and sweet expression, displays many of the features that make these dolls so desirable. She has a cork pate under her blond wig and applied ears. Her straight-wrist body was made by Schmitt, suggesting she may have gone to a dolls' hospital years ago where she had her body replaced, and this will lower her value. She is wearing contemporary clothes, and it is likely that her red hooded cape was made specially for her.
Height: 24in (61cm)
Value: $8,000–12,000

RIGHT When Émile Jumeau took over the running of the firm in 1876 he introduced his popular bébé. This wonderful all-original example dates from c.1880 and has the typical shaded lids, pale eyebrows, and closed mouth of the period. Her magnificent dress and hat are of silk satin trimmed with appliquéd rose sprays and she has matching earrings. Her particularly attractive clothes will add considerably to her value.
Height: 19in (48cm)
Value: $10,000–14,000

MARKS

• Earliest are unmarked.
• Early bébés impressed on the head with "EJ."
• After 1878 when Jumeau won a gold medal at the Paris Exposition, bodies carried a "Medaille d'Or" label in blue
• When Jumeau won a Diplôme d'Honneur in 1885 bodies carried a paper stamp printed "Diplome d'Honneur" in blue.
• Some later Jumeaus just have a red painter's mark on the back of the head.

DOLL	DATE	CHARACTERISTICS
Portrait or almond eyes *(size no. only)*	1877–c.1883	Pale-colored pressed bisque head, mauve shaded lids, eight ball-joint body, and straight wrists.
Long-faced *(size no. only)*	1878–1887	Sad, pensive expression, some with pale faces, often large 32in (81cm).
"EJ" bébé *(marked 'EJ')*	1881–1885	Heavy, chunky body, straight wrists, pressed bisque head, soft painting.
Later bébé *(marked Deposé Jumeau)*	1885–1887	Light eyebrows, pressed bisque, pretty dolly face, straight wrists, jointed composition body.
Tête Jumeau *(marked Deposé Tête Jumeau)*	1885–1899	Heavy brows, poured bisque, jointed wrists, closed or open mouth with teeth.

ABOVE The original clothes of this early pressed bisque bébé of c.1880 need some attention as they are suffering signs of wear and tear. Note the similarities in her colored socks and shoes to those of the doll above left, and the same finely-modeled hands on fixed wrists. Unusually for a French doll, this example has the English store stamp of Cremer and Sons, Regent Street, London, on her body.
Height: 18in (45.75cm)
Value: $8,000–12,000

ABOVE Although this doll is only 33cm (13in) tall, she has all the high quality features of the larger dolls, including a skin wig, pale pressed bisque head, and delicately painted features. She is an early unmarked Jumeau dating to the 1870s. The close up, with her wig removed to reveal the cork pate beneath, shows the mold line down the side of her face where the bisque, including the ears, has been pressed into the two-part mold. The forehead is unusually high but would have been covered by the wig.
Height: 13in (33cm)
Value: $5,000–7,000

ABOVE Although this doll from the late 1870s is very similar to the one on the right, the heavier brows and lashes significantly change the look of her face. She has been redressed, which will lower her value, but she is still a highly desirable doll. Like the doll on the right, she is marked only with her size number 3/0.
Height: 13in (33cm)
Value: $4,500–6,000

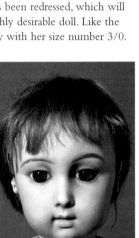

RIGHT Jumeau introduced its long-faced or *triste* bébé in 1877 and today it is one of the most sought-after dolls. Modeled by the sculptor Carrier-Belleuse, she is characterized by her sad, thoughtful expression and her very large eyes. Other features include the pierced ears applied after the pressed clay head was removed from the mold. This doll's lashes are long and delicate and two lip colors have been used to indicate the shape of her open/closed mouth. Her brown mohair wig is attached to a cork pate that fits into the head aperture. Her only mark, as with all dolls of this mold, is a size 15, but her jointed wood and composition body is stamped in blue with the post-1878 "Medaille d'Or" mark of Jumeau.
Height: 31in (79cm)
Value: $18,000–25,000

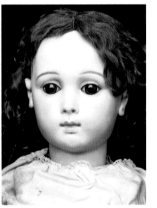

ABOVE Unlike the doll on the left, this otherwise very similar example has brown eyes and may be slightly earlier: her eyebrows are paler and there appears to be some shading on the eyelids.
Height: 31in (79cm)
Value: $18,000–25,000

ABOVE Different artists can give dolls a different face, even if the mold is the same. This late 1880s long-faced doll's heavy brows and tiny, deep pink pursed mouth make her look different from her sisters.
Height: 32in (81cm)
Value: $18,000–25,000

LEFT The box of this Tête Jumeau is stamped "Jumeau Medaille d'Or" indicating that it was made after 1885 when the firm won this award. There is absolutely no doubt as to this doll's maker as not only does she come in a labeled box, but she is stamped with the usual "Tête Jumeau" mark on the back of her head and even has a stamp on her shoe and another label attached to the sash on her dress! This is an indication of the prominence of the firm in the doll market during the 1890s and its attempts to take every opportunity to promote itself. Although the doll's dress is pretty, it is not of the high standard of the silk dresses that appeared on its dolls in the 1880s. She also has a more pronounced mouth than earlier dolls, with an exaggerated cupid's bow and upturned corners.
Height: 32in (81cm)
Value: $4,000-6,000

RIGHT The fact that this Tête Jumeau from the 1890s is still in its original factory-made simple cotton dress in excellent condition and has its original box, add to its value. She has the typical body of the later dolls, with jointed wrists rather than the fixed ones of earlier examples. Her mold number "1907" probably refers to her date of manufacture. Her open mouth suggests that her head was imported from Germany to fill the demand for Jumeau dolls in France. Today Jumeau bébés with open mouths, such as this, are less desirable than those with closed mouths. This doll was made after the amalgamation of the French factories into the SFBJ but when the individual factories still marketed their dolls under their own names and this also makes her less desirable than earlier dolls.
Height: 14in (35.5cm)
Value: $2,200-3,000

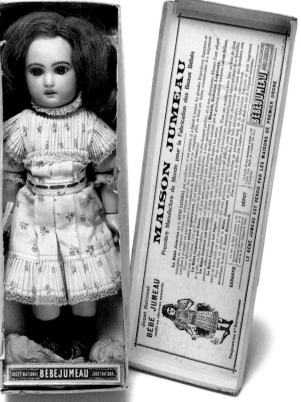

ABOVE Tête Jumeaus were introduced in 1885 and were so-called because of the stamp on the back of the head. The marks on this doll are typical. The letters "SGDG" signify that the doll was sold without the guarantee of the French government. The other mark, "HM," is that of the painter. This is one of the first examples and has the earlier body type with fixed wrists.
Height: 12in (30cm)
Value: $3,200-4,000

Steiner

Clockmaker Jules Nicolas Steiner established his doll-making business in 1855, specializing in walking and talking dolls. Although he ceded his firm in 1891, it continued to make dolls under various managers until 1902, the year of Steiner's death. He was probably the most innnovative French doll and toy maker, as his clockmaking training have him the ability to design many fascinating moving toys, and with his Series and Figure dolls, the variety of faces is infinite.

BELOW Steiner's waltzing doll was his second mechanical doll (the kicking doll on the right was the first), probably produced after his patent No. 57803 was granted in 1863 for a mechanical doll with a single pullstring. Her child-like face, pale coloring, light brows, and stationary neck also help to date her to the 1860s when these features were typical. When wound up, she glides along the floor on three wheels at the base. The front wheel can be angled to make the doll roll in a circle. As she moves she raises and lowers her hands and cries out "Mama" and "Papa." It is likely that her dress is original, as it is suitably childlike, although longer than normal so as to cover the cardboard skirt that houses her mechanism. This doll was such a success that it was made until the end of the 1890s. Later waltzing dolls have a more sophisticated adult look, higher face coloring, darker brows, and slimmer skirts, reflecting the change in fashion for more ladylike dolls.
Height: 15in (38cm)
Value: $3,000-5,000

ABOVE Steiner's kicking and crying doll, introduced in 1862 when Steiner was granted a patent for its *bébé parlant automatique*, was one of his clockwork dolls that was popular over a long period. Early examples made in the 1860s had German papier-mâché arms and legs and heads dipped in wax. Later, Steiner bought Paris-made bisque heads for the dolls, which have torsos made of a heavy cardboard covered in fabric. The dolls had an on/off lever at the hip as well as a winding mechanism. The baby was a delightful toy for a child to own.
Height: 20in (51cm)
Value: $2,200-3,000

ABOVE This undressed mechanical doll from the 1880s is displaying the more slender version of the cardboard skirt base that is found on the mechanical lady, far left. The key is similar to those of both the lady and the bébé. The head is possibly by Gaultier and the torso is heavy cardboard covered with kid leather. She has a swivel neck, more traditional for dolls of her period than the earlier rigid neck version, but she is not as pretty as her older sibling.
Height: 15in (38cm)
Value: $2,500-3,500

ABOVE Steiner made its Series C heads with open and closed mouths. This 1880s example has her original blond mohair wig. These dolls are called wire-eyed because of the wire lever at the side of the head that opened and closed the eyes.
Height: 16¼in (41cm)
Value: $4,500–6,500

ABOVE Steiner's Series A heads are very similar to those of his unmarked early bébés. They have particularly small mouths close to the nose, large expressive eyes, and often the pink cheeks of this 1880s example.
Height: 18in (46cm)
Value: $5,000–7,000

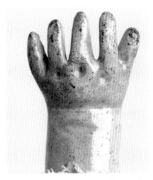

ABOVE Steiner hands from the 1880s are very distinctive because of their stubby fingers and knuckle indentations. The hand and lower arm are made in one piece, of a very light papier-mâché that was peculiar to Steiner. Where the paint has rubbed away at the joints it is often possible to see the deep violet color of the papier-mâché underneath.

ABOVE This mid-1870s bébé has the open mouth of Steiner's talking dolls, but no voice mechanism. Typical characteristics of early Steiners are the skin wig and strongly pronounced cupid's bow mouth.
Height: 16in (40.5cm)
Value: $4,000–6,000

ABOVE Steiner set the irises of some of his dolls' eyes into a special bisque eye ball which was less translucent than the glass eyes of most bisque dolls. The hazel eyes of this 1880s Series C head are very unusual.
Height: 28in (71cm)
Value: $7,000–9,000

ABOVE Steiner's 1880s Series E doll is very rare, and this one with its pink cheeks, alert expression, and pale, long eyebrows is particularly charming. Although rare, the painting is sometimes less precise than other molds, so its value has a wider range. Large examples command a premium.
Height: 10in (25.4cm)
Value: $10,000–15,000

ABOVE This splendid Figure C has a wonderful secretive smile. The brows are heavy and date the doll to the late 1880s or early 1890s. Her nose is typically wide and the blue wire-operated eyes are large. The fact that her modeling is so crisp suggests she was probably one of the first dolls of the mold and this together with the fine painting will add to her value.
Height: 22in (55cm)
Value: $6,500-9,500

ABOVE Steiner's innovative range of dolls included a number of male dolls, which are very rare today, doing adventurous things such as riding camels. This example, made in c.1899, was probably originally dressed as a soldier but is now wearing the clothes of a businessman. He has masculine heavy brows, large lustrous eyes, and an almost smiling mouth.
Height: 11in (28cm)
Value: $25,000+

ABOVE Steiner's Figure A doll was introduced in 1887 and marketed from 1892 as Le Parisien and is one of the most commonly found Steiner bébés. She was painted with many different expressions including this worried one. She has a lovely soft face which was also sold in other colors, including a mulatto doll, a black doll, and a white doll painted with red and black clown maquillage. Like the Series C on page 83, she was also made as an open-mouthed version.
Height: 25in (63.5cm)
Value: $5,000-7,000

RIGHT This large open-mouthed, unmarked talking doll has the typical body of Steiner's 1890s dolls, although her mechanism is operated by unusual brass levers. The Series C she is holding has the same early body but with the purple papier-mâché of the 1880s dolls. Typical features of the early bodies are the fixed wrists and short, stubby hands.
Height: large 23in (58.5cm); small 10in (25.4cm)
Value: large $10,000-15,000; small $5,000-7,000

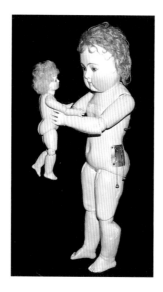

LEFT There are many variations of Steiner's Figure A dolls, although the face is always rectangular with full cheeks. This little lady, c.1890, is wearing her original clothes which will add to her value. The dolls show a striking resemblance to Jumeau's bébés (see pp.78-81) and reflect the competition at this time between these two major French doll manufacturers.
Height: 10in (25.4cm)
Value: $4,000-5,000

RIGHT This is one of the earliest Figure B dolls, made between 1887–88 and stamped with the early Bourgon mark on the back of the head. Her face is of a lovely translucent bisque and she has blue feathered paperweight eyes which have greater depth than some of Steiner's more innovative eyes. Her nicely made plush clothes are contemporary—possibly a copy of an outfit worn by her owner.
Height: 16in (40.5cm)
Value: $4,500–6,000

MARKS In 1889 Steiner registered its first trademark of a baby holding a flag which was stamped on the body of dolls from this time. Earlier dolls were usually marked on the back of the head with "J. Steiner" or "Sie" together with the series number and the size. The stamp on the left is from the Figure B doll to its left; the Petit Parisien bébé Steiner was also marked in this way. Figure Bs are hard to find; note that the heads always have an open mouth.

ABOVE Jules Steiner's designs extended to toys, including this very rare composition-headed acrobat modeled as an elegant performer with the mustache and small beard that was fashionable in the 1870s. He rolls along his tightrope by means of a wooden pulley positioned between his legs which moves them backward and forward in a running motion. As can be seen, this action has caused the composition on his feet to break off, leaving the metal foundation beneath. His carved wooden hands are carrying a balancing pole. He is still in his original clothes, although a little tattered now, and the fact that he is with his box, bearing Steiner's mark as well as that of the shop "M Delastang," will add to his value.
Height: 9in (23.5cm)
Value: $2,000–4,000

A BRIEF CHRONOLOGY

1862	Patent granted for *bébé parlant automatique*.
1862–1890s	*bébé parlant automatique*, waltzing doll and early bébé produced.
c.1870–1873	The first articulated body produced with separate ball joints.
1880–c.1887	Bourgoin takes over as toymaker at Steiner and his name appears on the mark during this time.
Early 1880s	Series dolls introduced, starting with Series A, although not following an alphabetical chronology. Feature traditional articulated body with purple papier-mâché used on dolls until the early 1890s, usually straight wrists and fat fingers, and until c.1889 some times marked with the Caduceus stamp
1887	Figure dolls first introduced, always marked on the body and the head. After c.1890 feature articulated body of grey papier-mâché and a more grainy bisque for the head.
1888–1890s	Ear with a canal features on Figure heads.
1889	Medaille d'Or awarded to Steiner; appears on marks from this time.
1890	Patent for *bébé premier pas* granted.
1890–99	Amédée Onésime Lafosse takes over company.
1892	Le Parisien trademark registered by Lafosse.
1899–1902	Jules Mettais takes over company.

Schmitt et Fils

Schmitt et Fils produced bisque and bisque-headed bébés in France from 1863 to 1891. The firm is best-known for its bébé which it produced from 1879 with three primarily different shaped faces—long, round, or square. It is interesting that Maurice and Charles Schmitt's first patent in 1877 was for decorating porcelain shoulder heads, proving that they were, in part at any rate, involved with the actual production of their dolls' heads. They were among the first makers of bébés, winning a silver medal in Paris in 1878. Their dolls differ from those by other makers in look and body shaping, yet remain relatively undervalued.

LEFT This lovely early Schmitt bébé from c.1880 has a round face, tiny mouth, and bulbous pale blue eyes outlined with a darker blue. She has a "cup and saucer" neck where the neck socket fits up inside the head, a very rare jointing method used by Schmitt which makes her even more individual. On her flat bottom—another characteristic of Schmitt dolls—she is typically marked with crossed hammers within a shield. It is important not to confuse Schmitt with the German dolls made by Franz Schmidt or Bruno Schmidt of Waltershausen.
Height: 12in (30.5cm)
Value: $10,000–15,000

RIGHT The fact that this wonderful Schmitt bébé is still wearing all her original clothes, including a high-quality satin and velvet dress, original underwear, and French shoes marked with the name of the London shop where was she was originally purchased, makes her a highly desirable doll. Her wrists are not jointed, a typical feature of French bébés in the 1880s.
Height: 15½in (40cm)
Value: $14,000–18,000

LEFT The longer face of this mid-1880s Schmitt bébé is attractive. Other differences from the doll above include the softly painted mouth with a lighter color between the lips, and her larger, more lustrous eyes. She has a mohair wig over a cork pate, whereas the doll above has a plaster pate. The jointed wood and papier-mâché body has separated fingers and the dress, although not original, has been made up of old materials.
Height: 17in (43cm)
Value: $8,000–12,000

François Gaultier

In addition to making bisque heads for fashionable dolls (see pp.68-9), François Gaultier made all-bisque dolls as well as heads for firms such as Rabery et Delphieu, Jumeau, Gesland, Thuillier, and Vichy. In 1899 the company joined together with SFBJ, and dolls made after this time are not of as high quality as early examples. The firm often marked dolls on the head with the initials "FG" and a size number, and even the later heads made by them with SFBJ carry the Gaultier mark.

ABOVE The heavy brows and full mouth of this Gaultier bébé head are typical characteristics of dolls of the 1890s when she was made. Earlier Gaultier bébés had fine eyebrows. Although she has lustrous, large brown eyes surrounded by long painted eyelashes, the detailing is not as sensitively carried out as on earlier dolls, and her single lip color is less subtle. She has her original long mohair wig and a jointed wood and papier-mâché body.
Height: 24in (61cm)
Value: $3,000-4,000

ABOVE These two Gaultier bébés are marked with the initials "FG" within a scroll, which dates them to after 1887 when this new mark was introduced. They both have jointed metal Gesland bodies with composition limbs. The doll on the right is of higher quality, with a closed mouth, paler bisque, and more subtle coloring. Typical Gaultier characteristics include the round cheeks and small, pointed chins. Although the dolls are redressed in old clothes, the fact that they have their original wigs is important to their value.
Height: left: 24in (61cm); right 26in (66cm)
Value: left $3,000-4,000; right $4,000-5,500

Other French Bébés

There were many small firms making dolls in Paris during the third quarter of the 19th century. Most of these did not have their own porcelain factories, and ordered the heads for their dolls from bisque producers such as François Gaultier (see p.87). However, it is likely that firms had their own molds, as there is a great variety of features among the dolls of different makers and the quality differs vastly. At the top end are the dolls made by A. Thuillier in the 1880s and at the bottom end are the poorer quality later dolls of Etienne Denamur.

Each doll maker created its own body types and wigged and dressed their dolls in fashionable Parisienne clothes. The most expensive dolls had complicated outfits made of satin and velvet, cheaper dolls wore pretty dresses of stiffened muslin and cotton lace. With the less expensive dolls, condition is particularly important to the value, and those in poor condition will always be much less desirable.

RIGHT Musical dolls, known as Folies or Marottes, produced a tune when their handle was twirled. The dolls are usually German, but this example has a French shoulder head marked with the Gaultier cartouche. It has a closed mouth, bulbous eyes, mohair wig, and the typically French turquoise earrings. Most of these musical rattles are dressed in this type of costume, with pointed lappets decorated with lace or braid and ending in bells. As this is a good quality toy, the handle is of turned bone and incorporates a whistle at the base.
Height: 12in (30cm)
Value: $700-1,500

FAR RIGHT Jesters, or Punchinellos, were very popular in the 19th century. Many illustrations of toy stores show them hanging outside their windows. They are often found with composition character faces with hooked chins and noses but this is a very superior bisque example, with a head that may have been made by Gaultier or Jumeau in the 1880s, as it is similar to those of their fashionable dolls (see pp.68-70). He is loosely jointed so that he can move his bisque arms and legs freely in a humorous manner befitting a jester, and he is still wearing his brightly-colored satin parti-colored clothes.
Height: 11in (28cm)
Value: $1,500-2,200

ABOVE This very rare bébé marked "2/0 JM" is by a maker who has not yet been identified, although some collectors believe the mark to be that of Jules Mettais. Dating to the late 1870s, she has the typical skin wig over a cork pate, shaded eyelids, pierced ears, closed mouth with a lighter space between the lips, and a jointed wood and papier-mâché body with straight wrists. She is wearing an appropriate wool and velvet dress with braid decoration to the belt and hem which although not original is contemporary with when she was made.
Height: 15in (38cm)
Value: $8,000–15,000

ABOVE The firm of Étienne Denamur advertised their bébés as being less expensive than those of other makers. This example, impressed "ED," certainly looks so, with rigid limbs, unimaginative modeling, and sparse painting. She has a mohair wig, unattractive open mouth, and the obligatory pierced ears of French dolls made at the end of the 19th century.
Height: 15in (38cm)
Value: $600–1,000

ABOVE Danel et Cie was set up by ex-Jumeau director, Danel. Jumeau successfully sued him for using his molds and tools and for head-hunting his fellow workers. This doll, made by Danel et Cie in the 1890s, has a red stamp on the back of the neck reading "Paris-Bébé Tête Deposé 10." Made to celebrate the building of the Eiffel Tower, the body of these dolls was often stamped with a picture of this famous landmark.
Height: 22in (55cm)
Value: $3,500–5,000

LEFT Bayeux et Mothereau made dolls in Paris between 1880 and 1895. This early example, marked "B4M," is particularly unusual as she has a metal body, which is now showing through the worn paint. The upper arms and legs are wood. Other similarly marked dolls have the same long, soft eyebrows, exaggerated cupid's bow lips, and large lustrous eyes. Other makers such as Dumoutier and Madame Huret used metal parts for their dolls.
Height: 15in (38cm)
Value: $12,000–18,000

SFBJ

The foundation of the Société Français de Fabrication de Bébés et Jouets in 1899 was the French response to the dominance of the doll market by the Germans and was the start of the decline in the quality of French bisque-headed dolls. Initially, the two major partners were the Jumeau factory and the German commercial investor Fleischmann & Bloedel. Later, smaller partners joined, including Girard, Bru, Gaultier, and one of the main manufacturers of porcelain heads, Pintel and Godchaux, although their contributions of money and premises were of secondary significance.

SFBJ dolls tend to be of lesser quality than earlier French bisque dolls. Some still bore their former firm's marks, such as Jumeau and Eden Bébé, but the names of many of the most famous makers all but disappeared.

SFBJ introduced their own 200 series of character dolls in 1910, and these charming, childish faces were generally of higher quality and were better finished than their 301 or 60 "dolly" face models. SFBJ continued to make dolls into the 1930s and the fact that they produced a vast number of inexpensive dolls means that it is possible for many collectors to have at least one French bisque doll in their collection.

ABOVE In 1938 SFBJ produced two dolls, France and Marianne, for Queen Elizabeth and King George VI to give to the Princesses Elizabeth and Margaret. The original pair were 31½in (79cm) high, but SFBJ soon made this commercial example which was only 20in (51cm) and wore an organdy dress.
Height: 20in (51cm)
Value: $1,500-2,500

LEFT The mold 252 character doll, know as "*le boudeur*" or "the pouter," is one of the most desirable SFBJ molds and is exceptionally well-modeled and life-like, with curious bumps on the forehead and a protruding upper lip. This c.1912 example has no painted upper lashes, but retains the remains of fur lashes on her slightly sunken sleeping eyes. This head is usually found on a bent-limb baby body with a distinguishable separate big toe.
Height: 24in (61cm)
Value: $4,500-5,500

This close-up of the face of the doll on the left details the unusual sleeping eyes and the molded teeth visible through parted lips which are typical features of these dolls.

The SFBJ mark is impressed on the nape of the neck. Collectors should examine dolls of mold 60 carefully as they vary greatly in quality. Many of the 11in (28cm) size, called *Bluette*, were sold through the magazine *La Semaine de Suzette*, which issued patterns weekly for the doll's clothes.

The wood and composition body parts are strung together with elastic. This elbow joint is a typical example.

LEFT The effect of the solid irises of SFBJ dolls is evident in this c.1910 child doll whose eyes look strangely black. She is damaged on her legs and hands and the dark color is showing underneath the paint. The composition bodies of these dolls are usually darker than those of German examples, and they tend to be slimmer. Despite the damage, she is nevertheless desirable because she is wearing her original white dress, socks, and shoes.
Height: 15in (38cm)
Value: $350-650

ABOVE This c.1900 mold 60 is a typical example of the dolly faced dolls SFBJ produced. Indications of lesser quality include the short, badly-proportioned arms and the basic face-painting. Many SFBJ dolls that survive today are no longer wearing their original dresses; this example is wearing a dress made of antique fabric copying a traditional design, but she still has her original shoes and brown mohair wig.
Height: 16in (40.5cm)
Value: $350-650

German White Bisque Shoulder Heads

The Germans followed the French in making bisque-headed dolls in the 1860s because a more flesh-like texture could be achieved than with the earlier china heads. When choosing a bisque shoulder head, look for interesting hairstyles, well-painted features, and extra details such as glass eyes, hair ornaments, or molded clothing. Most were made entirely in Germany and have stuffed cotton bodies attached to bisque arms and legs, but heads were also exported without bodies, particularly to the United States. Some were sold as heads only and put on home-made bodies, while others were given commercially made bodies. Both are considered "original." Factory or store-made clothes are rare, but add enormously to the value of the doll. Most heads represent women or older children. Hairstyles and footwear offer the most accurate clues to dating. High-heeled boots first appear after 1865 and tassels at the front of the boot were fashionable in the 1870s. The marks of some of the best makers, among them Simon & Halbig and Bahr & Proschild, appear on some shoulder heads and these are particularly desirable.

LEFT This somewhat fat-faced but well-made doll is difficult to date. Although her hairstyle first came into fashion in the 1850s, her molded boots have little heels, which did not appear on dolls until 1865. She is of good quality white bisque and has delicately painted features. Her hands are bent outward in a similar manner to those found on Kling dolls from the 1880s (see p.95). Her home-made dress is of printed cotton but has the type of full skirt found in the late 1850s. Assuming that her arms are original, one could guess at a date of 1880, bearing in mind that old parts were often used on new dolls and that home dressmakers were not necessarily high fashion seamstresses! Another indication that she was made in the 1880s is the pigeon-breasted shape, a feature of some German dolls of the 1880s.
Height: 26in (66.5cm)
Value: $450–600

LEFT The shape of this woman's head is interesting, as the ringlets, which come from the crown in a severe line, have produced an almost triangular effect. Although this hairstyle, in a softer version, was fashionable from 1865, dolls with ringlets were made until the end of the century and sometimes even later. Perhaps this was because mothers and nannies have always favored tight curls for their little girls' hair. Shirley Temple is a 1930s example (see p.40), and some children even in the 1950s still went to bed in curlers to achieve those long, fascinatingly springy sausage curls their mothers loved. This doll's arms are nicely formed and her contemporary home-made dress of checked silk gives her an air of confidence.
Height: 15in (38cm)
Value: $300-450

ABOVE The tight curls arranged at the front of this girl's head, held back by a molded blue ribbon, date her to the 1890s, when this style was popular. Her face painting is delicate, with the typical tiny mouth of these dolls, but the fact that her limbs are fairly crude and she wears a home-made dress trimmed with a harsh too-wide blue ribbon to match her hair, will detract from her value.
Height: 15in (38cm)
Value: $250-500

ABOVE Shoulder heads rarely survive in such good condition as that of this lovely girl from the 1860s. Although unmarked, she is of the high quality of the dolls made by Simon & Halbig, with molded decoration including a blue Alice band, a bow and flowers, gilded earrings, and a delicate necklace. Her long, elegant limbs are finished with molded, tasselled boots with the fashionable black toes of the period.
Height: 18½in (47cm)
Value: $1,500-2,500

ABOVE. The molded and gilded hairstyle of this doll is noteworthy, with its distinctive pink luster tasselled cord which falls over one side of her head, and an ostrich feather, often painted green but in this case white, on the other side. Her face is long and thin, giving her an aristocratic hauteur, and she has sloping shoulders. Her long, shapely limbs and flat-heeled boots, suggest a date earlier than 1865. Also helpful when trying to date this doll is her original ivory satin evening dress delicately trimmed with artificial flowers.
Height: 7½in (19cm)
Value: $800–1,200

ABOVE. This fine shoulder-head of the 1870s was possibly made by the same maker as that of the doll on the left, as the delicate features are very similar, and the beautifully-styled hair is just as elaborately decorated, secured at the back with a gilded ribbon and bow. She is in good condition, although unfortunately one of her earrings has suffered some wear. She has a typical German body of a type that would have been attached to china and bisque shoulder heads of this time. Her legs have the characteristic molded heeled boots.
Height: 16in (41cm)
Value: $600–900

HAIRSTYLES

As with china heads (see pp.56–61) studying the hairstyles of German bisque heads can help in dating a doll, although some styles, particularly ringlets encircling the head, were produced over a long period and are hard to date. One indication is the quality of production, which tended to deteriorate toward the end of the century. Many of the dolls had elaborate hair nets, or snoods, like the one featured here. Sometimes they were painted a color different from the hair. Gilded ribbons, bows, flowers, feathers, earrings, necklaces, and collars are all particularly sought-after and glass eyes are more desirable than painted ones.

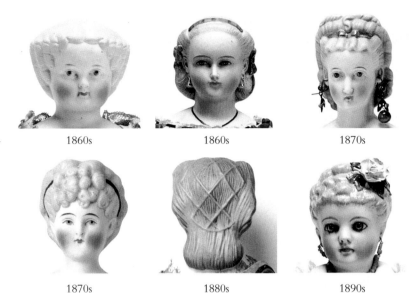

1860s   1860s   1870s

1870s   1880s   1890s

ABOVE A young immigrant to the United States, this German bisque shoulder head is attached to a typical American body with long brown leather arms. She is wearing a patriotic silk dress of the period and was probably made in 1876 to mark the centennial celebration of the signing of the Declaration of Independence.
Height: 18in (46cm)
Value: $650–900

ABOVE The inset blue glass eyes bring the face of this fine-quality C.F. Kling and Co. shoulder head to life and give her a child-like charm not found on the painted-eye dolls. Unusual for the time she was made (the 1880s), she has kid arms; most dolls by this period had bisque limbs. Her dress is not of the period.
Height: 18in (46cm)
Value: $700–1,000

ABOVE German-made dolls depicting other nationalities, or dolls representing a certain trade are good records of social history. This c.1910 Highlander is wearing his original, factory-made soldier's uniform, including molded spats. His complete Scottish regalia enhances his desirability.
Height: 10in (25.4cm)
Value: $150–250

GERMAN BISQUE

A number of German bisque dolls' heads were made in the 1860s, but by the 1870s the use of bisque had expanded rapidly and lovely shoulder heads with or without molded hair were made in great quantities.

Initiailly, small porcelain factories around Sonneberg produced the heads, very few of which were marked, and then sold them to doll makers who attached a body and clothes. But as the business grew, established doll makers and new firms used bisque heads for their dolls. When bébés first appeared in France (see pp.74-91) at the end of the 1870s and beginning of the 1880s, similar child-like faces appeared on shoulder-heads made in Germany. The quality of the doll was determined by the porcelain factory where the head was made and factories such as Kestner and Simon & Halbig who produced beautiful dolls, were commissioned by other doll makers to make heads to their own specification or design. The dolls were usually fine and the prices low and by the 1900s the German market had outstripped the French, exporting huge numbers of dolls to Europe and the Americas.

After 1890, when importing countries demanded that the country of origin should be marked on the doll, doll makers also added their own names and often the mold number and size, and it is these marks that are so useful to collectors today.

When buying German bisques look for crisp modeling (that is to say, from a new mold), careful, detailed, sensitive painting, and pale bisque without impurities.

Kestner & Co.

Kestner is one of the oldest doll manufacturers in the world, founded by Johannes Daniel Kestner in 1805. The earliest dolls were made of turned wood, but by the 1840s the firm made dolls with papier-mâché heads and kid or cotton bodies with wooden limbs. In 1860 Kestner bought a porcelain factory in Ohrdruf and started producing dolls with china and bisque heads and composition bodies under the name of Kestner & Co. The earliest dolls are difficult to identify as they were not marked, but by the 1880s the distinctive Kestner quality and look began to appear and dolls were marked with a mold number on the back of the head and sometimes the initials "J.D.K." As in other firms, the big change in production came with the introduction of character dolls in 1909, and many of the characters they created are outstanding. Their dolls, which are of consistently good quality throughout the range of sizes they made, are popular with collectors. In 1930 they merged with Kämmer & Reinhardt (see pp.103-5).

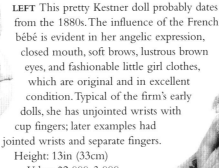

LEFT This pretty Kestner doll probably dates from the 1880s. The influence of the French bébé is evident in her angelic expression, closed mouth, soft brows, lustrous brown eyes, and fashionable little girl clothes, which are original and in excellent condition. Typical of the firm's early dolls, she has unjointed wrists with cup fingers; later examples had jointed wrists and separate fingers.
Height: 13in (33cm)
Value: $2,000-3,000

ABOVE RIGHT The 150 mold number of these two small all-bisque, fixed head dolls is impressed on the joints. The smaller doll is also stamped with a paper crown on its stomach—one of several Kestner marks used. The larger of the two dolls is of higher quality, with more delicate painting and a very pretty contemporary dress decorated with red cherries. Usually these small dolls were sold naked, so the quality of their clothes varies enormously. The blue of their painted socks is common.
Height: left 8in (20.5cm); right 6½in (17cm)
Value: left $400-700; right $300-500

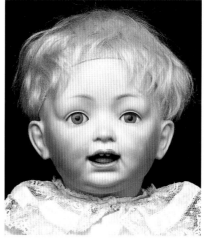

ABOVE Although this rare c.1912 bonnet head baby does not have a mold number, it is very similar to the 247 character doll. The molded lacy bonnet is trimmed in pink, but others were trimmed with blue. The Kestner baby body has the typical upturned big toe.
Height: 15in (38cm)
Value: $10,000–15,000

ABOVE Kestner was one of the few companies to produce both heads and bodies. A distinguishing feature of the dolls is the plaster dome to which the wig is attached; most firms used cardboard. This c.1912 mold 226 has a baby body, fine modeling, and an appealing look.
Height: 20in (51cm)
Value: $800–1,400

ABOVE Typical characteristics of Kestner's mould 221 googly-eyed dolls, first made in c.1910, are the round side-glancing eyes moved by turning a lever at the back of the head, short slanting high eyebrows, small snub nose, and "watermelon" mouth, painted only on the bottom half.
Height: 15in (38cm)
Value: $4,500–6,000

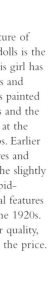

RIGHT A typical feature of Kestner's all-bisque dolls is the painted detailing. This girl has painted stocking tops and barred shoes. She has painted rather than glass eyes and the body is jointed only at the shoulder and the hips. Earlier dolls had sleeping eyes and were fully jointed. The slightly open mouth and cupid-shaped lips are typical features of Kestner dolls of the 1920s. However, she is poor quality, which is reflected in the price.
Height: 8in (20cm)
Value: $300–450

LEFT Some later heads made by Kestner for other companies show a deterioration in quality. From the 1920s the firm made Walküre dolls for the German firm of Kley and Hahn. This example is impressed "250 KH Walküre 3 1/4 Germany." Dolls of this type were often sold only in a chemise, shoes, and socks; this example is wearing a later satin dress. She has straight wrists and a jointed wood and composition body and has the brown sleeping eyes typical of many of the dolls made by Kestner.
Height: 23in (58.5cm)
Value: $450–700

ABOVE Kestner character babies have many distinguishing features. This c.1910 baby is typical, with its open/closed mouth, sleeping glass eyes, original five-piece baby body, and distinctive bent left arm. The head of this example is marked with Kestner's initials and the size number 14, but no mold number.
Height: 17in (43cm)
Value: $700–1,200

LEFT Kestner made a number of four-headed doll sets which are very rare today. They came in two sizes with three character heads. This set consists of molds 187, on the doll, and 180 and 186, plus a dolly face (mold 171), all in a cardboard box. These characters have painted eyes and the dolly face sleeping ones. To change the face the socket head was removed from the body and replaced with another. Some sets have been split up and the Kestner heads attached to other bodies.
Height: doll with head 17½in (44.5cm)
Value: $12,000–20,000

Simon & Halbig

The Simon & Halbig factory at Gräfenhain in Thuringia was set up in 1869 to produce porcelain products of an exceptionally high quality. It quickly moved on to making dolls' heads for the growing industry in the area. From its early shoulder heads with finely molded hair, painted or inset glass eyes, and bisque arms and legs, to the later socket heads with "dolly" or character features, the standard of design and execution was extraordinarily high. Quality was maintained even on its tiny dolls' house dolls and all-bisque dolls. Many other manufacturers and wholesalers ordered heads and body parts from Simon & Halbig, including Adolf Hülss, Adolf Wislizenus, Franz Schmidt & Co., Catterfelder Puppenfabrik, Louis Lindner & Söhne, and Heinrich Handwerck. From 1902 Kämmer & Reinhardt had all their dolls' heads made by the factory.

Many of Simon & Halbig's dolls' heads are impressed with its name and the name of the wholesaler they were made for, reflecting the esteem in which the firm was held by other doll makers. Those they exported to France do not bear their mark, but later SFBJ heads and red-stamped "Tête Jumeaus" impressed with "DEP" are thought to have been made by Simon & Halbig. The firm remained in business making high-quality dolls until the 1930s.

RIGHT Simon & Halbig made a number of Oriental girl dolls although unlike many other German makers, it did not make Oriental babies. Because of their fine modeling and elaborate clothes they are highly collectible today. These two, dating to c.1912, are both mold 1199 but the variations in size, color, and painting give them a quite different look. The girl on the left has been redressed in a costume which is a little big for her and will lower her value, although this is compensated for by her bigger size; the girl on the right still retains her original outfit.
Height: left 15in (38cm); right 13½in (34cm)
Value: left $1,600-2,200; right $1,600-2,500

RIGHT Early child dolls, such as this 1890s mold 949, have a domed shoulder head attached to a kid body rather than the later flat head with a cardboard pate. This example has a closed mouth, but the same mold was also made with an open mouth, although as with most dolls, the closed mouth version is more desirable.
Height: 20½in (52cm)
Value: $800–1,500

LEFT This mold 1260 dolly-face 1925 shoulder-head doll is dressed in her original blue muslin dress trimmed with lace. Her shoes and socks are a matching blue, as is the hair ribbon on the side of her almost untouched luxurious blond mohair wig. Her body is of pink kid rather than the pale cream of the doll below, but her arms are of the usual jointed composition.
Height: 13in (33cm)
Value: $450–750

ABOVE This very rare and early topsy-turvy doll was made by Simon & Halbig in the late 1870s/early 1880s. With a flip of her skirts, the finely-modeled howling faced doll transforms into a sweetly smiling girl. She has molded blond infant's hair and is wearing her original red silk outfit, decorated with gilt metal stars, lace and metallic braid, and bells. When you turn over her skirts her outfit changes to a pale turquoise blue. A very unusual doll, her all-original and excellent condition will also add to her value.
Height: 6in (15cm)
Value: $2,200–3,000

LEFT This flirty-eyed mold 1250 doll has the German jointed kid body attached to a bisque shoulder head typical of dolls introduced in the 1880s. It is of high quality with ball and pin joints at the elbows where it joins the bisque and "*ne plus ultra*" and "universal" joints at the hip and knee which allow the doll to sit up and bend her legs. Her lower lip has a characteristic dark red triangle. Flirty eyes are less frequently found and add to her value.
Height: 18in (46cm)
Value: $600–1,000

RIGHT In contrast to the doll on the right, there has been no attempt to create ethnic features on this c.1910 mold 1079 doll. Simon & Halbig have simply taken a standard dolly face and painted it brown. The firm made a vast number of highly collectible brown dolls, but early unrealistic molds such as this are less expensive than later ones.
Height: 20in (51cm)
Value: $700-1,200

LEFT In its later ethnic dolls, Simon & Halbig managed to create ethnically accurate features, rather than just simply reproducing a white mold in a different color. This lovely mold 1358, has the correctly modeled face of an African child; and the use of the open mouth with a row of porcelain teeth is very appealing.
Height: 22in (55cm)
Value: $6,500-9,500

LEFT This mold 117 doll came dressed either as a boy or girl, and with a child's body. This sweet girl is appropriately dressed, as at the time she was made—in 1912—most little girls wore crisp white pinafores over their dresses to keep them clean. She has a mohair wig, introduced on German dolls in the 1880s, and blue sleeping eyes.
Height: 18in (46cm)
Value: $4,500-6,000

ABOVE Simon & Halbig made a series of Lady dolls in the 1900s; this mold 1159 has great presence. She still has the label of "Au Nain Bleu" in her hat, for the Paris toy store which probably produced her elaborate Edwardian pink silk and embroidered tulle afternoon dress. Her body is that of an adult, with fine shaping.
Height: 24in (61cm)
Value: $2,200-3,000

"DEP 1249" describes a mold with a "dolly" face and an open mouth. "DEP" is for "Deponiert," which translates as "deposit," indicating that a patent has been applied for. The number 5 refers to the size of the doll.

LEFT Simon & Halbig made this mold 1249 doll for Hamburger and Co. in 1900. It bears the "Santa" trademark by which it became known. It is a very popular mold as although it has a dolly face, the quality of the painting is unusually high and the mouth is painted with two colors and has sweetly upturned corners, giving her a smiling expression.
Height: 14½in (37cm)
Value: $650–950

This head shows the double marks of Kämmer & Reinhardt and Simon & Halbig and the mold number 117/A.

On some dolls' heads made by Simon & Halbig for Kämmer & Reinhardt, such as the back shown here of the head of the 114 Hans doll on p.106, only the mark of Kämmer & Reinhardt appears.

RIGHT This mold 100 doll was made by Simon & Halbig for Kämmer & Reinhardt in 1909. It was the first in a series of character dolls, and is one of the easiest to find today. Subsequent designs continued to be numbered from 100 (for example, 114, 117, and so on). This particular doll was popular as its face is different from the usual "dolly" face of the time, and was supposedly modeled on a real baby from an orphanage. The eyes are painted and the mouth is open, but with no hole cut into the head (called "open-closed"). The head is a solid dome with hair indicated by a few brush strokes. This example has the characteristic outstretched arms, with one shorter than the other, and legs arranged in a sitting position. From this mold followed all the other character dolls designed by Simon & Halbig and the other German and French manufacturers.
Height: 14in (36cm)
Value: $500–800

LEFT A rarer, brown version of the 100 baby is shown here. Although Simon & Halbig did also produce dolls with ethnic features (see p.102), for these character dolls (c.1909) it used exactly the same mold as for the white baby. The darker hue seems to give the baby a more attractive face, although the color can be quite uneven. Some examples were also produced with even darker skin than that of the doll here.
Height: 14in (36cm)
Value: $1,000–1,400

BELOW This small mold 117A girl is a favorite with collectors. Made in c.1912, she has a closed mouth and, unlike most character dolls, has sleeping eyes of the type used by Simon & Halbig from the mid-1880s. However, she has the short single stroke eyebrows typical of their painted eye character dolls. She was made for Kämmer & Reinhardt in a variety of sizes. This example is only 11⅓in (29cm) high, but even in this small size there has been no compromise on quality.
Height: 11½in (29cm)
Value: $2,200-3,000

LEFT Simon & Halbig's character molds provide an infinite variety for the collector. This c.1910 mold 109 girl has a cheeky face, with eyes glancing slightly to the left and just the semblance of a smile. She has her original wig with the typical center parting of Simon & Halbig's dolls. Her dress is home-made, but appropriate in style. Unfortunately, she has lost a number of her fingers, which detracts slightly from her value.
Height: 18in (46cm)
Value: $8,000-12,000

ABOVE Mold 114 was made by Simon & Halbig for Kämmer & Reinhardt in c.1910 either as a girl called Gretchen or as the boy on the right, named Hans. They were made by a different sculptor from earlier molds and were modeled on Franz Reinhardt's grandson.
Height: 17in (43cm)
Value: $4,500-5,500

ABOVE The rather petulant, expression lends itself well to being dressed as a boy. Hans is not wearing his original clothes, but they are at least contemporary to the doll, and reflect the fashion at the time of always wearing a hat out-doors! Dolls in original clothes command a premium.
Height: 17in (43cm)
Value: $4,500-5,500

ABOVE The sleeping eye mechanism of Simon & Halbig's dolls can be seen clearly here. There is a piece of cork at the bottom of the wire which prevents the lead weight from striking against the bisque and breaking it.

ABOVE The method of setting stationary eyes is illustrated here, with a layer of plaster applied inside the head to hold the eyes in place.

ABOVE The wig of this mold 114 doll has been removed to reveal the blotchy painting around the rim and evidence of the vegetable glue used to attach the wig to the head. The mold for the eyes is clearly visible.

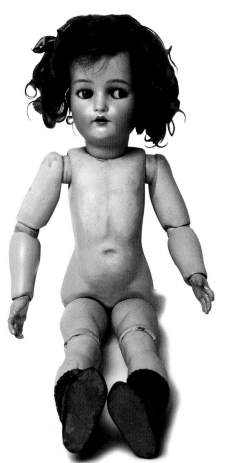

ABOVE This dear little baby character mold has a bent-limb baby's body, original short mohair wig, and a lovely silk robe. As with the mold 116A, above right, the 115A mold above was made as a 115 version which has molded hair rather than a wig. It is interesting that the Kathe Krüse doll 1 of 1909 (see p.130) is very similar in design, as is the Schoenhut spring-jointed baby of this time (see p.24), probably because they are all based on the 16th century 'Fiamingo' head of a child by Dutch sculptor François Duquesnois.
Height: 15in (38cm)
Value: $3,000-4,000

ABOVE This little dimpled girl, mold 116/A, is attached to a nicely modeled toddler's body with diagonal hip joints. Her pretty hand-made silk clothes were made either at home by a dressmaker, or for a store when the doll was made, c.1912. A 116 version of this doll had molded hair rather than mohair and is valued slightly higher.
Height: 16in (40.5cm)
Value: $2,500-3,500

LEFT The fine modeling of this body is typical of Simon & Halbig/Kämmer & Reinhardt's later dolls. The upper and lower arms are of turned wood. She has a slight waist indicating she was made as a child rather than a toddler. The ball joints are separate pieces at the elbow and knee, but are part of the limbs at the shoulder and hip.
Height: 20in (51cm)
Value: $80-1,000

Gebrüder Heubach

The Heubach factory was a porcelain plant based in Thuringia that made bisque figures as well as attractive and amusing character dolls. The brothers Heubach bought the factory in 1840 and production continued until the Second World War. While their sunburst trademark was registered in 1882, dolls with this mark date to the early 20th century. Although all Heubach dolls are marked with a mold number, this is often difficult to read today. However, the heads are often stamped with two pairs of numbers in green, a system unique to Heubach which helps in identification. Another feature unique to some Heubach heads is the use of a bisque colored pink throughout. Even though the firm's heads are sometimes attached to poor-quality jointed composition or pink cotton bodies, this will not detract from the desirability of rare molds with fine modeling.

LEFT Gebrüder Heubach is famous for its character dolls with their variety of unusual and expressive faces. Examples that are whistling, pouting, or winking are particularly collectible. These two date to c.1912. The boy at the front is unusual as although modeled as a young baby, he has molded curls.
Height: 12in (30.5cm) each
Value $500-750 each

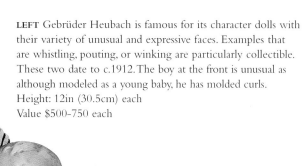

RIGHT This charming, coquettish little girl looking out of the side of her eyes is a favorite with collectors. She has a normal little girl's jointed composition body and a home-made blue cotton dress edged in lace. Not all Heubach characters carry a mold number, but this doll is impressed with Heubach's square mark and the mold number "77 88." Gebrüder Heubach was also famous for its bisque figures and many of them share very similar faces to their dolls, suggesting that the same modelers worked on the figures and the doll heads. A distinguishing feature of both are the expressive intaglio eyes.
Height: 13in (33cm)
Value: $700-1,000

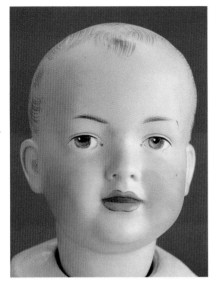

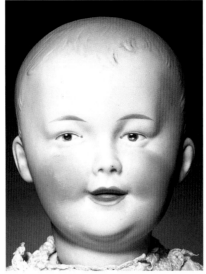

ABOVE This character mold is similar to mold 76 02, but the pout has turned into a partly open mouth with the hint of a tongue showing. A dark line above the eye touches a red dot at the inner corner and continues down just past the eye at the outer corner. There are no eyelashes, but a light red line is painted to indicate the fold in the eye, and the eyebrows have a quizzical look.
Height: 18½in (47cm)
Value: $1,000–1,400

ABOVE This unusual character doll, mold 76 47, has the intelligent expression that is found on many of Gebrüder Heubach's character children, particularly its pouty dolls, but here the expression makes him look a little older than the molded-hair baby he represents. He has the characteristic intaglio eyes and smiling open/closed mouth of many Heubach characters.
Height: 18in (46cm)
Value: $1,500–2,500

ABOVE This head with its molded bonnet is known as Baby Stuart after a portrait of Charles the First's children, in which the baby prince is wearing a similarly shaped cap. It comes in several versions, including socket heads and one with a removable cap.
Height: 15in (38cm)
Value: $1,500–2,200

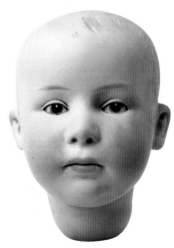

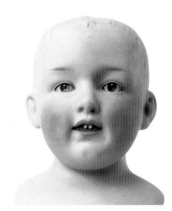

LEFT This baby head has almost identical features to that of the bonnet head, above right, with a down-turned mouth and intaglio eyes. In this example the hair is lightly molded and painted blond. Although not visible in this picture, there is a bisque loop attached to the base of the neck of the doll for fastening it to a body.
Height (head): 4in (10cm)
Value (head): $400–600

RIGHT Although Gebrüder Heubach heads are usually of very high quality, they are often attached to poor-quality bodies. This shoulder head of c.1914 with an open/closed mouth is usually found on a pink cotton body stuffed with reindeer hair, often with black legs to indicate stockings, and inexpensive composition arms.
Height (head): 4in (10cm)
Value (head): $350–500

Armand Marseille

Russian-born Armand Marseille emigrated to Germany, where he set up a porcelain factory in Köppelsdorf in 1885. From 1890 he started to make dolls and became one of the most prolific doll-makers in Germany. He is most famous for his Dream Baby dolls, made between 1924 and 1938, among the most popular dolls ever produced, and subsequently copied by other manufacturers. Because the same dolls were made over a long period of time, dating can be difficult. Their quality varies, even within the same mold number, and collectors should look for examples that are well-modeled and painted and with bodies of good-quality composition. The rare molds are particularly sought-after, although the more common dolls are popular as they provide the opportunity to have a collection of bisque dolls for a relatively low price. Production ceased in 1930.

LEFT With its soft features and high-quality painting, mold 1894 (possibly the year the doll was first made), is one of the most sought-after of Armand Marseille's doll-faced dolls and is harder to find than some, like the prolific 390 on p.110. It came on a variety of bodies, including one with a composition chest, stuffed to mid thigh, and wooden lower legs. This doll is very well-painted and it is a shame her eyebrow has been marred by the firing. She is impressed "1894 AM 5 DEP, made in Germany."
Height: 19in (48cm)
Value: $400–550

LEFT This is a mold 1894 of lesser quality than the one above, with less clearly molded features and less expressive painting details. However, because she is still wearing her original clothes her value is higher. Made in c.1900 she is wearing matching dress and bloomers decorated in *broderie Anglaise* and the typical black stockings worn by little girls at the turn of the century.
Height: 19in (48cm)
Value: $450–600

ABOVE Molds 341 and 351 were made to represent African as well as white babies, but with no attempt at changing the features. This example is a lovely doll with a glow to the bisque and a nicely detailed and preserved dark composition body. His striped rompers are not original but look very sweet on his little fat body.
Height: 12in (30.5cm)
Value: $350–500

ABOVE and ABOVE RIGHT Armand Marseille's Dream Baby was made as mold 351 with the open mouth of the two babies here and as a more desirable closed mouth mold 341 version. It was made in a variety of sizes and with two main body types: the bent-limbed composition body of the baby on the left or the cheaper cloth version of the baby on the right, which here has celluloid hands; some were made with composition hands. It is quality rather than the date that affects the value.
Height: 14in (35.5cm) each
Value: left $250–350; right $175–275

RIGHT This c.1925 mold 353 baby, is actually modeled as an Oriental child, whereas the Dream Babies were simply painted a different color. Popular with collectors, it has a slightly flatter, wider nose than white versions, and typically Oriental slanted elongated eye sockets with wide upper lids. The hair on these babies is always sprayed on and there is no attempt to make it look realistic with brush strokes like some of the higher quality character babies made by Kestner. The skin has a yellow tint to it, particular to Armand Marseille's dolls.
Height: 16in (40.5cm)
Value: $900–1,200

RIGHT This c.1900 3200 mold is an example of the lesser quality dolls produced by Armand Marseille. Her bisque shoulder head is attached to a poor-quality stuffed cotton body with integral black stockings and disproportionately small, short white bisque arms. Her mohair wig is a replacement and she is not wearing her original clothes, which will devalue her further.
Height: 15in (38cm)
Value: $150-250

LEFT Armand Marseille seems to have supplied special order dolls to large department stores. One Edinburgh store in the 1930s sold all its fairy dolls clothed in the same pale green dresses, made in several sizes but all from Armand Marseille's 390 mold. This fairy, also mold 390 and from the same period, is wearing her original white butter muslin clothes trimmed with tinsel and lucky horseshoes. Because so many of these dolls were made, they are relatively inexpensive today.
Height: 12½in (32cm)
Value: $200-300

LEFT and FAR LEFT Mold 390 is the most common Armand Marseille doll, made in vast quantities from 1900 to 1938. They vary greatly in quality, with the best examples being finely modeled and painted with jointed composition bodies, and the least desirable having over-simplified features and straight legs. These dolls have survived in large numbers and it is quite easy to find one in good condition. Shown here are two typical examples both in their original clothes. The c.1907 doll on the far left is made of better quality bisque than the c.1900 doll on the left and has more detailed painting on her lips, giving her a less stunned appearance than that of her companion.
Height: left 22in (55cm); far left 15in (38cm)
Value: left $300-450; far left $350-600

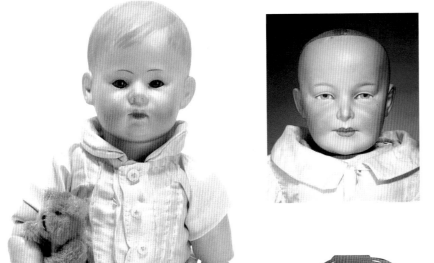

LEFT At first glance this head does not look like the work of Armand Marseille as it has flat painted blue eyes with intaglio pupils and a closed orange-colored mouth outlined in darker red, which are quite different from the features of their other dolls. However, the doll is marked "A6M" and is one of a series known to have been made by Armand Marseille without a mold number.
Height: 19½in (49.5cm)
Value: $9,000–10,000

LEFT Armand Marseille made this attractive googly-eyed mold 323 girl in c.1913. Her original regional costume covers her poor-quality rigid limb body and sadly, her face is badly cracked, which will greatly reduce her value. Even if she were to be restored she would not achieve the value of the same doll in perfect condition.
Height: 6in (15cm)
Value: damaged $200–300; perfect $650–900

ABOVE Among the most collectible Armand Marseille dolls are the rare mold 230 Fany dolls. This c.1912 Fany has a closed mouth, sleeping eyes, molded short hair, and a jointed toddler body, and lends himself well to being a boy. Another version with a wig, mold 231, makes an adorable girl and is even more popular with collectors.
Height: 12½in (32cm)
Value: $3,200–4,000

Other German Bisque

At the beginning of the 20th century when the German toy industry was at its peak, there were hundreds of firms making dolls for export. Some copied the designs of successful factories such as Simon & Halbig, Kestner, and Armand Marseille; many others produced good quality dolls, sometimes with unusual molds. A few of these smaller firms commissioned the heads and designs from the major porcelain factories and the quality of modeling and painting is comparable to that of the best makers. However, be aware of cheaper copies of a known mold. If the molding and painting are poor, although you recognize the features, the likelihood is that it is not by a major factory. Dolls made by the smaller firms are fun to collect and unless they are exceptional can be bought for a fraction of the cost of those made by the major makers.

ABOVE In 1906 Cuno and Otto Dressel registered the trademark Jutta for a line of dolls, many of whose heads were made by Simon & Halbig. This little character, marked "Jutta 1914," has been carefully made and nicely painted. It has painted lashes above its sleeping eyes, a quivering tongue, a mohair wig, and a typical baby's body. The long white robe, although not original is contemporary and suits the baby well.
Height: 18in (46cm)
Value: $600–800

RIGHT Cuno and Otto Dressel was formed in 1789 and, under the strict demarcation laws of the period, was permitted to work only as a wholesale house and not as a factory. It commissioned and bought dolls from other makers and was instrumental in the huge export business in the German toy industry throughout the 19th century. It exported lovely wax-over-composition dolls, composition headed dolls, and wooden-jointed dolls from Sonneberg, where in 1843 it founded the Sonneberg Federation of Trade. The smooth, dry glaze of this Cuno and Otto Dressel character doll is very rare and unusual; most had an unglazed finish.
Height: 16¼in (41cm)
Value: $5,000–7,000

LEFT Erste Steinbacher Porzellanfabrik is one of the many German doll manufacturers who made baby-faced bisque dolls that were very similar to those of the greatest manufacturers. This girl from c.1912 has an impressed mold number 23 and carries the "E St. P" mark of the company, but she bears a striking resemblance to the baby dolls made by Ernst Heubach of Koppelsdorf (see p.115).
Height: 17in (43cm)
Value: $225-350

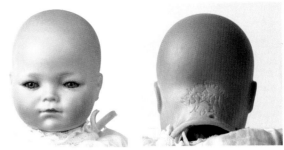

LEFT Schoenau and Hoffmeister Porzellanfabrik, set up by Arthur Schoenau and Carl Hoffmeister in 1901, produced both porcelain and bisque heads. One of their most popular designs is this Princess Elizabeth with a smiling mouth, sleeping eyes, and what were once golden curls.
Height: 18in (46cm)
Value: $1,200-2,000

BELOW and ABOVE This mold produced by Schoenau and Hoffmeister in c.1911 always has an especially fine, almost silky finish and is of higher quality than many of their dolly faces. The sleeping eyes are small in relation to the head and, together with the high, domed forehead and absence of any hair, give the impression of a very young baby. It has a stuffed body and composition hands.
Height: 15in (38cm)
Value: $700-1,000

RIGHT Schoenau and Hoffmeister probably made this desirable character doll called Hanna in the 1930s as she has the high coloring of the dolls of that period. This was also the time when many dolls were made with names (such as Princess Elizabeth, above, and Viola). Hanna has an appealing, laughing mouth, nicely shaped teeth, and distinctive eyebrows. The head was made at the firm's porcelain factory at Burggrub, Bavaria, hence the doll's mark of the initials "SH" with "PB" (Porzellanfabrik Burggrub).
Height: 18in (46cm)
Value: $600-800

RIGHT Catterfelder Puppenfabrik purchased heads from outside porcelain factories and as a result many of its dolls are very similar to those of the more famous makers. This c.1916 doll is nicely-made, with a head probably by J.D. Kestner and is impressed "CP 263 50."
Height: 20in (51cm)
Value: $600-800

LEFT Although the head of this 1920s Catterfelder Puppenfabrik doll was made by Kestner and has a distinctly Kestner-type look, with a protruding upper lip and heavy brows, she would not command quite the same price as a doll made entirely by Kestner and with Kestner marks, as her body is less expensive, with its stick-like upper limbs and small hands. She is a mold 502 dolly face and is impressed "Catterfelder Puppenfabrik 1."
Height: 17in (44cm)
Value: $450-750

ABOVE Theodor Wendt was a doll exporter based in Hamburg. This small mold 210 character baby, probably made by the firm in the 1920s, is not very high quality. His composition body has pink lines painted between the fingers and the toes and he has a replacement dark hair wig.
Height: 9½in (24cm)
Value: $125-200

ABOVE Porzellanfabrik Mengersgereuth made this mold 914 character child in the 1920s. It marked its heads with the initials "PM" but, like others, made heads for other makers, including Gebrüder Ohlhaver. This doll has a molded tongue joined to the lower lip, sleeping eyes, and a typical composition baby's body.
Height: 18in (46cm)
Value: $300-550

RIGHT C. M. Bergmann led a checkered career. Having emigrated to the United States where he had several jobs he eventually returned to Waltershausen and later set up his own doll factory. He specialized in ball-jointed composition bodies with heads bought in from a number of manufacturers including Simon & Halbig. He maintained his link with the United States by supplying toy stores in New York with his dolls. At 27in (68cm) high this mold 1916 dolly face is large enough to be dressed in the life-sized baby's clothes she is wearing, although they are not really appropriate for this style of doll.
Height: 27in (68cm)
Value: $600-900

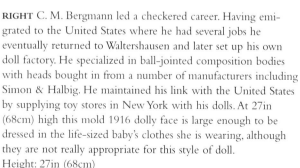

ABOVE Ernst Heubach of Koppelsdorf made a wide range of inexpensive bisque dolls in the 1880s before merging with Armand Marseille in 1919 to form the Koppelsdorfer Porzellanfabrik. Many of Ernst Heubach's later dolls have the rosy cheeks of this mold 267 baby made in the 1920s, and share her typically lively modeling. She has flirty eyes and a composition baby's body and is dressed in a home-made cream wool hooded cape and dress.
Height: 14in (36cm)
Value: $300-500

ABOVE Ernst Heubach's dolls are impressed "Heubach Koppelsdorf" and should not be confused with the higher-quality dolls of Gebrüder Heubach (see pp.106-7). This well-modeled c.1920 mold 399 doll has good ethnic features and sleeping eyes. She was fired in unpainted white bisque and the black flesh color and facial details were painted on later. This was cheaper than firing in the color and the doll was therefore not expensive despite its quality and large size.
Height: 20in (51cm)
Value: $200-300

ABOVE A. H. Schalkau designed this sad googly-eyed boy for Ernst Heubach in c.1911, together with a happy version. The six upper eyelashes on each lid are a lovely detail, giving even more individuality to the face. He retains his original short mohair wig and a well-modeled rigid limb toddler body. He is impressed with both names, "Heubach Koppelsdorf 319 5/0" and "A.H. Schalkau D.R.G.M."
Height: 11in (28cm)
Value: $4,000-6,000

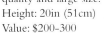

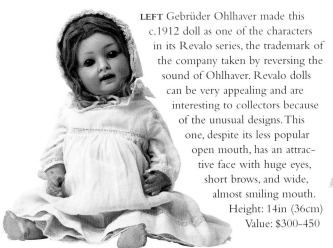

LEFT Gebrüder Ohlhaver made this c.1912 doll as one of the characters in its Revalo series, the trademark of the company taken by reversing the sound of Ohlhaver. Revalo dolls can be very appealing and are interesting to collectors because of the unusual designs. This one, despite its less popular open mouth, has an attractive face with huge eyes, short brows, and wide, almost smiling mouth.
Height: 14in (36cm)
Value: $300-450

LEFT Bähr and Pröschild's porcelain factory at Ohrdruf near Sonneberg produced good-quality dolls from the 1870s. It also supplied heads to other makers including Bruno Schmidt, who took over the running of the factory in 1918. This lovely c.1912 character baby has a delightfully-modeled face and it is always nice to find a doll such as this in all-original condition with a charming baby's body and elaborately decorated dress, cape, and hat.
Height: 11in (28.5cm)
Value: $500-800

ABOVE Franz Schmidt of Georgenthal in Thuringia began making dolls in c.1890 and was the first to make character babies with sleeping eyes. Heads were supplied by, among others, Simon & Halbig, who probably made the head of this c.1910 rare character doll who shares the fine modeling of the Kämmer & Reinhardt 100 series.
Height: 19½in (49.5cm)
Value: $15,000–20,000

ABOVE Franz Schmidt made this clockwork walking doll at the beginning of the 20th century. The metal body contains the mechanism that makes the tin plate legs move backward and forward. "Patent aller Lander" is stamped on the base of her boot, which means "patented in all countries."
Height: 12in (30cm)
Value: $600–900

ABOVE The firm of A. G. Limbach was founded in 1772. Its dolls were very popular in the early 20th century but their quality had deteriorated by the 1920s when this dolly face with her rosy color, orange lips, and coarse wig was made. She is impressed with "Wally 2" and the Limbach clover leaf mark.
Height: 17¼in (44cm)
Value: $175–250

LEFT Alt, Beck & Gottschalck had their own porcelain factory and were an established doll-making firm, founded in 1854. By the 1880s they were exporting large quantities of dolls' heads to the United States. The face of this 1920s mold 1352 rosy-faced flirty-eyed character is that of a baby or toddler but the head is on a fully-jointed child body (not shown).
Height: 17in (43cm)
Value: $300–450

LEFT This lovely Alt, Beck & Gottschalck mold 639 shoulder head is turned to the right, a feature found on shoulder heads of various materials in the 1880s and 1890s. She has fixed blue eyes, a mohair wig, and quite a large adult type kid body with separate fingers. Her dress is not original.
Height: 23in (58cm)
Value: $700–1,100

LEFT It is not known who made this lovely German dolly face, but the design was registered by George Borgfeldt & Co. She was probably a special order for his importing business, as similar dolls were advertised by him in 1908. She has a modern dress and a luxurious wig.
Height: 20in (51cm)
Value: $300-500

LEFT The Bye-lo Baby was designed by Grace Storey Putnam, a teacher in California who copyrighted her design for the doll in 1923. George Borgfeldt & Co. produced this example, with a soft baby-like body and standard celluloid hands, in the late 1920s. The Bye-lo Baby was one of its most popular dolls and was later made by others including Kestner and Alt Beck & Gottschalck.
Height: 12in (30.5cm)
Value: $400-700

BELOW Theodore Recknagel made many character dolls and babies from 1910 to the 1920s that were often loosely based on the designs of other makers but, with a few exceptions, of lesser quality. This baby doll has tiny eyes and a rosebud mouth which has been made to look small by not paying attention to the lip line during painting. The jointed composition body with fixed wrists is in fact of better quality than the head. It is impressed "Germany 3 ½ R 138 A."
Height: 15in (38cm)
Value: $350-600

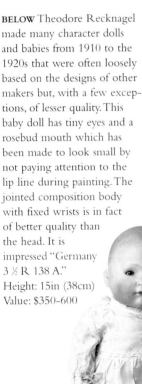

LEFT The Kewpie doll was designed by American illustrator Rose O'Neill who patented her Cupid-like character in 1913. The high quality of this example dating to the 1920s suggests it was made for the American market by the Kestner factory, which started making the dolls in 1913. They were then distributed by George Borgfeldt. The figures continued to be made in many different poses, costumes, and materials by a number of manufacturers until the 1970s, many with the Rose O'Neill signature on the foot. Notable features are the starfish hands, little blue wing buds on the shoulders, a pointy tuft of hair, and huge side-glancing eyes. The most desirable Kewpies are those modeled with costumes, such as firemen, or in unusual poses or in groups.
Height: 4in (10cm)
Value: $150-250

RIGHT William Goebel produced many amusing character dolls from c.1910 including brightly-painted babies with googly eyes. He had his own porcelain factory and made heads for his own dolls and for other manufacturers. Although the firm was founded in 1867, its dolls were never of the quality of those of such firms as Simon & Halbig and Kestner. This cheerful little man has sleeping eyes with lashes and his original mohair wig. He has a composition bent-limbed baby body and is dressed in a contemporary home-made knitted outfit.
Height: 16in (40cm)
Value: $350-450

LEFT This beautifully-modeled character doll with a closed mouth and painted eyes is something of an enigma but is sometimes attributed to Hertel Schwab. He bears the mold number 111-7 with no maker's mark. This is similar to Gebrüder Kühnlenz's dolls which also had a two-number mark with a hyphen between the mold and size. He lacks some of the subtlety of Kämmer & Reinhardt's characters, but is a very rare doll with a lovely face.
Height: 12in (30.5cm)
Value: $6,000-9,000

ABOVE William Goebel made this "American schoolboy" character boy with large eyes and molded hair in c.1912. His bisque shoulder head is attached to a gusseted kid body with bisque arms.
Height: 19in (49cm)
Value: $600-900

LEFT This doll is marked in the same way as the boy on the left, and is impressed with the mold number 111-4. She has glass eyes instead of his painted ones, which bring her face to life and give her a sweet, pensive expression, and her eyelashes and eyebrows are nicely-painted. Her good-quality jointed body is dressed in a lace dress. This doll is of exceptional quality and the 111-4 mold is a very rare one and this, combined with the fact that she is very pretty, make her a highly desirable doll.
Height: 16¼in (41cm)
Value: $15,000-20,000

ABOVE The beautifully-made real hair wig of this 1860s untinted bisque shoulder head, arranged in a plaited, coiled bun at the nape, is particularly high-quality. The wig was attached to a black circular patch on the pate of the solid-domed head, which is a common feature of bisque and china shoulder heads. She has a slight smile on her face, pale pink lips, an aquiline nose, and a red painted line above her blue painted eyes. It is very rare to find these elaborate wigs in such good condition because they are extremely fragile.
Height: 10⅝in (27cm)
Value: $500-700

ABOVE Clown toys were very popular from the 1880s to the start of the First World War when circuses made regular performances. This white-painted untinted bisque clown head has a flange neck which suggests it was made for a mechanical or moving toy.
Height: 2½in (6cm)
Value: $50-75

ABOVE This doll is a typically poor copy of Kämmer & Reinhardt's 100 series (see p.103), and was probably made by Wiesenthal Schindel and Kallenberg. The modeling is not as crisp and the quality of the bisque and the painting are inferior.
Height: 11in (28cm)
Value: $200-300

LEFT Although the modeling of this unusual c.1912 character boy is good, the execution and painting are poor in comparison with that of some of the best makers. He has painted hair on his solid domed head rather than a mohair wig (hidden under his woolen hat) and a poor quality stuffed body with composition arms. He is not marked with a maker's name, only "Made in Germany 205 6/0" and is probably by Gebrüder Knoch.
Height: 17in (43.5cm)
Value: $200-300

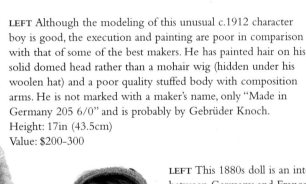

LEFT This 1880s doll is an interesting example of how the trade between Germany and France existed at the end of the 19th century. Her flat-domed head is of high-quality pale German bisque and has two holes through which string is threaded, joining it to the body. She has an open/closed mouth, stationary blue striated eyes, and a mohair wig. However, her body is French, made of turned and painted wood with composition feet. Her hands are of a pewter-like substance which can be seen where the paint is flaking off. This type of body was used by Petit et Dumoutier of Paris who may well have imported the head, painted in the French manner, to make up the doll. Her clothes are new, but she is still a lovely doll to have in a collection.
Height: 22in (56cm)
Value: $2,500-3,500

CLOTH DOLLS

Cloth or rag dolls are probably the most traditional of all types of doll, made at home since the earliest times from simple materials. Few survived, but in the 19th century, several American women, among them Martha Chase and Izannah Walker, in small home workshops, began to produce commercially-made cloth dolls with painted faces and great charm, and these survive in small numbers today. At the end of the 19th century and the start of the 20th, printed cloth designs were produced, enabling children to make a doll for the price of a few pieces of material and a bit of stuffing, although because they were usually made from only two or three pieces, they often had little realism or movement. In 1909 Käthe Kruse produced her beautifully painted and extremely realistic Doll 1 with five leg seams. Steiff also produced good-quality jointed dolls, although some considered the center face-seam unattractive. Soon other firms in Europe started making cloth dolls, including Lenci, Farnell, Chad Valley, and Dean's.

Unlike their bisque contemporaries, cloth dolls were sold dressed and prices are seriously affected if clothes are missing, dirty, or damaged. Lesser firms emulated the work of the greater ones and collectors should be aware of this, for although they are collectible, these dolls will not command as high prices.

LEFT (left to right) A 1920s felt Steiff boy doll; a 1960s Dean's Golly; and a 1930s Chad Valley Bambino doll in original dress and wig.
RIGHT (left to right) Two painted cloth dolls by Martha Chase of Rhode Island and a c.1920 Käthe Kruse Doll 1 in original clothes.

Izannah Walker

Izannah Walker from Central Falls, Rhode Island, made dolls probably from the 1850s and first patented her designs in November 1873. She pressed together in molds layers of inexpensive cloth covered in glue to form the head and facial features. When dry a layer of padding was added, covered in stockinette, and then painted with the facial and hair details. The shoulder heads were attached to gusseted fabric bodies. Izannah's painting is reminiscent of that of the itinerant portrait painters of the period and her skill at creating simple charm makes her dolls very endearing. They are very rare, particularly outside the United States, and when they appear, command a premium.

This close-up of the face shows the typical Izannah features, including painted ringlets (other examples had wisps or curls of hair painted on the face), applied ears, large brown eyes, and a closed mouth.

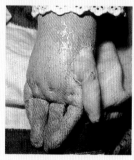

The hands of Izannah Walker's dolls are very distinctive with a separately stitched thumb.

ABOVE This group of five Izannahs shows the variety and size of dolls she made. The large doll at the back is an early prototype and has the characteristic painted, tight ringlets of many of the dolls; the four smaller ones, all dating from the 1870s, were once played with in the home of the Walker family.
Height: 27½in (70cm) to 8½in (21.5cm)
Value: $5,000-12,000 each depending on condition

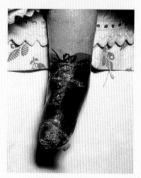

Typically feet had painted boots with laces painted on; less common are bare feet with molded toes.

Martha Jenks Chase

Stockinette-covered children and babies were made by Martha Jenks Chase and later by her family from 1889 until the late 1930s. They were sturdy dolls, the faces and limbs painted in glowing oil color. The heads were made by placing a mask under the stockinette, and they had painted, molded hair. The firm also made teaching dolls for childcare work, totally oil-painted so they could be immersed in water. The dolls were labor-intensive to produce and were more expensive than imported bisque dolls, yet demand appears to have been high and they often appear on the market. They were sold dressed and undressed, some as characters in *Alice in Wonderland* or as George Washington. The black adults and children are more sought-after and expensive than white children as they are much rarer and dolls with unusual hairstyles also command a premium.

ABOVE These two oil-painted cloth dolls are typical of Martha Jenks Chase. The 1910 larger doll has short blond hair, brown painted eyes, a sateen covered body, and oil-painted lower limbs. The smaller 1920s doll has bobbed hair and blue painted eyes. Height: left 13½in (34cm); right 16½in (42cm) Value: left $1,200-1,800; right $600-900

ABOVE This large black mammy from c.1930 is holding a small white 1920s baby in her arms. She has molded and painted facial details, and unlike many of the dolls of German bisque manu-facturers, her features are distinctly ethnic. Height: mammy 26in (66cm); baby 14in (35.5cm) Value: Mammy $7,000-12,000; baby $500-800

RIGHT Early Chase bodies from 1910 to the 1920s, such as the one shown here from the doll on the left, have seams at the knee, hips, elbow, and shoulder. Later ones were jointed only at the shoulder and hip.

BELOW Chase dolls had a label sewn onto the body (on this example attached to the doll's back) and a printed stamp which here is on the top of the leg. Dolls that still have their labels fetch a higher price.

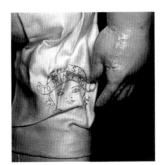

Other American Makers

Because the United States was still a new country in the 19th century, with no long-established industries, most luxury goods had to be imported, including dolls. Women soon took to making them themselves out of cloth, the most notable being Izannah Walker and Martha Jenks Chase who set up home industries to produce dolls that today are highly sought after (see pp.122-3). But by the early 20th century, the American toy industry was burgeoning, and many firms used cloth for dolls.

Always look for exmples in good condition and with attractive faces. Rag dolls such as Babyland Rag by Horsman and printed cloth dolls by such firms as Art Fabric Mills of New York are fun to collect. But generally dolls with all-over printing are less expensive than those with printed or painted faces, jointed bodies, and separate clothes, which cost more to buy at the time they were made. Nineteenth-century American cloth dolls have escalated in price over the last few years. They hold enormous historical importance for American collectors and with their naive charm are eagerly sought-after. Very few were exported and they are rare outside the United States.

RIGHT The Albert Brückner Company was founded in Jersey City, New Jersey, in 1901. It produced a number of topsy-turvy dolls, including one which featured a mohair teddy bear on one side and a ragtime female dancer on the other. With a flip of the skirts this example changes from a black doll to a white one, both dressed in identical gingham dresses. It is a later version of a very popular doll first made by Brückner in 1901 (the label below dates it to the 1930s), and the faces are no longer as pretty.
Length: 12in (30.5cm)
Value: $450-600

ABOVE It is interesting to compare this Brückner mammy with the black topsy turvy doll on the right as they are identical, even down to the red bow in the hair. The mask faces were first printed and then three layers of material and paper were compressed to form features.
Height: 10½in (26cm)
Value: $600-900

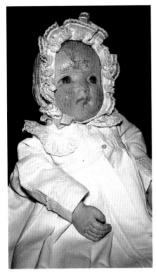

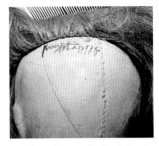

ABOVE Louise R. Kampes made dolls from her studio in Atlantic City, New Jersey, between 1919 and 1928. The dolls were originally sold wearing delightfully simple children's clothes of the period and attractive hats, but these two have lost theirs! There are close similarities to the dolls made by Käthe Kruse. Typical Kamkins features include the flange neck, body jointed at the hips and shoulders, mohair wig, and painted cloth head. The earlier doll on the left here has a fully-painted disc-jointed body and is marked on the head (as shown); the later doll on the right has an unpainted body and swing limbs. These later dolls were marked with a paper heart carrying the words "Kamkins, a dolly made to love," but few of them still have the label today.
Height: left 19in (48cm); right 19in (48cm)
Value: left $1,400-1,800; right $800-1,400

ABOVE Martha Wellington of Brookline, Massachusetts, probably made this stockinette baby with an oil-painted face in the 1880s. It is very similar in style to the Philadelphia baby on the right, with a finely-modeled upper lip and nicely defined hands. These dolls are very rare.
Height: 23in (58cm)
Value: $10,000-14,000

BELOW This Kreuger Kewpie doll can be dated to the 1950s because of the nylon material covering its body. It carries the mark of Kewpie's creator, Rose O'Neill and of Kreuger.
Height: 8in (20cm)
Value: $75-90

ABOVE Philadelphia babies were produced exclusively for the J.B. & Co. Sheppard store in Philadelphia in c.1900. They had cloth bodies and molded and painted stockinette faces, lower arms, and lower legs. This lovely example, Harry, is dressed ready for school, complete with teddy, violin, and bag full of marbles; on his lapel is a star pin for winning a three-legged race. The dolls are typically well-painted with soft skin tones and strong features.
Height: 20½in (52cm)
Value: $3,500-5,000

BELOW This Snow White and the Seven Dwarfs made by Richard Kreuger of New York in the 1950s is one of a number of sets of the popular Disney characters made at this time by, among others, Chad Valley and Merrythought.
Height: Snow White 15in (38cm)
Value: $1,400
the set

Primitives

Although primitive dolls were made in other parts of the world, those from the United States excite the most interest today. In a rapidly growing country where people lived mainly on the land and had little spare money and few things to spend it on, parents made their children's toys themselves. It is these home-made dolls, mainly dating from the 19th century, that are of so much interest. They vary greatly in quality of execution, as some mothers were more adept at sewing or painting than others. Although many collectors regard them as old, ugly rags, they are important historical documents and should be treasured as such. More than any other kind of doll, their provenance is particularly important. The circumstances of when and where they were made and by whom are as important as the doll itself and the information should be attached to and remain with the doll. Native American dolls or black dolls are especially interesting, the former also appealing to collectors of ethnographical objects.

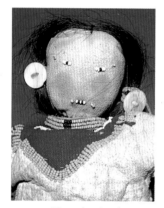

ABOVE Note the simple gentleness in the features of this hand-made Native American Crow woman from c.1880, where just a few beads can create an interesting expression.
Height: 13½in (34cm)
Value: $3,000-5,000

ABOVE The face of this primitive cloth black woman from the 1880s has white button eyes, an applied nose, and embroidered mouth. Although not shown, her body is cloth, with kid hands.
Height: 21½in (54.6cm)
Value: $600-800

ABOVE This group of three home-made primitives shows the variety made in the United States at the turn of the 20th century. The lady on the left has a particularly flat face, with hand-painted features. She comes with a note that says she was made in 1907 by Eva Rowe Crawford of Gloster (*sic*), Mass., for her granddaughter. In the center is a minstrel from a house in Maine. One of a kind, he probably dates from the 19th century. The man on the right is all-knitted, copied from a pattern in *Harper's Bazaar* in 1892.
Height: left to right 18in (46cm), 20in (51cm), 15½in (40cm)
Value: left to right $800-1,200, $1,200-1,800, $300-500

RIGHT This extremely appealing primitive cloth doll from the 1880s has oil-painted features and is wearing a wonderful cotton plaid bathing dress which she has hooked up to show her bloomers!
Height: 18in (46cm)
Value: $1,800-2,500

LEFT Made in Eastern Massachusetts in c.1930, this little girl with knobbly knees has Cornrow-type braids tied with red ribbons to match her short dress. She has applied ears, needle sculptured, white oilcloth eyes outlined in black embroidery, and appliquéd nose and mouth with beads inserted for teeth.
Height: 17½in (44.5cm)
Value: $500-600

RIGHT A note in the pocket of this charming hand-made primitive from the last quarter of the 19th century says she answers to the name "Sweetie," and she certainly looks a loyal and trustworthy friend.
Height: 17in (43cm)
Value: $800-1,200

ABOVE These twins are based on the Dickens character, Dolly Varden. Made from 1906 to 1912 and distributed by Butler Brothers, they have lithographed faces over cloth and wear their original clothes.
Height: 14in (35.5cm) each
Value: $250-350

ABOVE These home-made cloth twins are identical, but one has a drawn face and the other a painted one, suggesting the artist possibly ran out of time or enthusiasm. Dressed in identical red cotton dresses, each carries a paper doll with a story book in its hand. Occasionally pairs of dolls surface, often made or dressed for sisters, with only small differences such as hair or eye color. These have been tucked away in a trunk since 1860.
Height: 17in (43cm) each
Value: $2,000-3,000 the pair

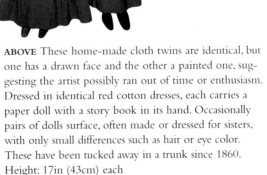

Steiff

The famous firm of Steiff was founded in 1877 and although it is primarily known for its exceptionally high quality teddy bears, it also made a wide range of felt toys in the 1900s. Margaret Steiff, crippled by polio as a child and confined to a wheelchair, started making felt toys from remnants in a local toy factory and produced her first animal—a felt elephant pincushion—in 1880. With her nephew Richard she soon established a highly successful business which continues to produce toys to this day.

Many Steiff dolls are character figures, such as the policeman in Beatrix Potter's *Two Bad Mice,* and characters from comic strips and children's books. As moths can badly damage cloth and the clothes are so important to a cloth doll, those in good condition fetch disproportionately more money than a poor example. The children are perhaps the most delightful, but the other characters tend to be rarer and are undervalued when compared with later cloth dolls by other makers.

RIGHT To find a complete set of Steiff cloth dolls is exceptional and this c.1910 Village School will command a premium, particularly as the dolls are in such excellent condition and come complete with writing desks, satchels, slates, books, blackboard, and teacher. The dolls all have lovely smiling faces and are wearing their original clothes. Steiff made a number of sets of this popular toy which was perhaps used to prepare children for school. Examples were also made by other makers in different materials. Height: teacher 17in (43cm); pupils 10-12in (25.4-30.5cm) Value: $10,000-20,000 the set

RIGHT Many of Steiff's dolls were based on famous characters, or were caricatures of types; this very rare composition-headed example is modeled as a local militia man and seems to reflect the popular idea that small local military units were full of country bumpkins! Only three examples of this doll have been found, all wearing identical uniforms but with different comical faces. This one is missing his cap and shoulder bag but the fact that he is so rare will add to his value.
Height: 12in (30.5cm)
Value: $2,000-3,000

LEFT Many companies made military and patriotic toys and dolls during the First World War and Steiff was no exception. This example is dressed as a German infantryman and comes complete with equipment, guns, and the traditional German helmet.
Height: 15in (38cm)
Value: $1,200-2,000

LEFT This boy displays all the typical characteristics of Steiff's felt dolls including:
• a vertical stitched seam down the center of the face
• black button eyes
• painted eyebrows
• large feet in proportion to the body
• stitched mouth
• a mohair wig
Like all felt toys, Steiff dolls are susceptible to damage, particularly moth holes, fading, and dirt, and those in perfect condition will command a premium. Unfortunately this boy has lost his original clothes and his hands have been repaired—originally he would have had cotton stitching to represent his fingers. He is very similar to a doll called Anthony, distributed by George Borgfeldt in the United States and made by Steiff in 1909. As with Steiff bears, all Steiff dolls had a button tag in their ear.
Height: 10in (25.4cm)
Value: $400-600

Käthe Kruse

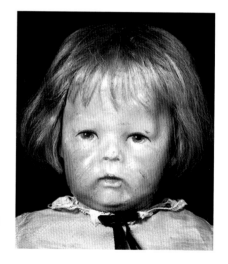

Käthe Kruse was born in Breslau, Germany, in 1883. She became an actress at 17, but after meeting Max Kruse, a Berlin sculptor, she gave up the stage for motherhood and a Bohemian life in the Swiss countryside. When Max refused to buy bisque-headed dolls for their daughters, Käthe made her own dolls, using a towel filled with sand for the body and a potato for the head. Her designs became more sophisticated and by 1910 she had enlisted Max's help in sculpting a head for a doll she presented at an exhibition of homemade toys in Berlin. Her dolls were so successful that she commissioned Kämmer & Reinhardt to manufacture her designs. However, Käthe soon started making them herself with a few workers. From this humble beginning grew the factory at Bad Kosen that was to make Käthe Kruse a household name. Her cloth dolls are among some of the most collectible and expensive today, especially those in original clothing and whose painting is still in good condition.

ABOVE Käthe Kruse commissioned the Kämmer & Reinhardt factory to manufacture her first doll design. They made her doll for only a short period in 1911 as she was not pleased with the quality and soon switched to making the dolls herself from her workshop in Bad Kosen. The rare doll on the left shows the quickly-rejected model, which has unusual cloth ball joints, arms akimbo, and a short, fat body. The doll on the right is the Bad Kosen version of Doll 1, this one made in the 1920s. Note the more realistic body shape and relaxed arms. Doll 1 was the only model made by Käthe Kruse until 1922. Because the Kämmer & Reinhardt doll is so rare it commands a premium. Height: left 14in (36cm); right 16½in (40cm) Value: left $5,000-7,000; right $3,500-4,500 dressed, $1,500-3,000 naked.

ABOVE Käthe Kruse started making this wigged version of Doll 1, known as Doll 1H, in 1929. Although not visible in the picture, this example has the typical wider body of their early dolls. A later model introduced in 1938 had the characteristically slimmer body of later Kruse dolls. Height: 17in (43cm) Value: $4,500-5,500

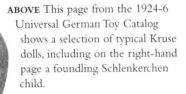

ABOVE This page from the 1924-6 Universal German Toy Catalog shows a selection of typical Kruse dolls, including on the right-hand page a foundling Schlenkerchen child.

LEFT Käthe Kruse started making this sand-filled Du Mein baby-craft teaching doll in 1925 and continued to make it until the 1950s. This example came in a box which had a list of necessary baby clothes typed on the lid. The baby's body was filled with sand to make it a realistic weight and a floppy head and navel added to the realism. This is one of the later examples, probably made in the 1950s.
Height: 20in (50cm)
Value: $3,500-4,500

ABOVE The influence of Käthe Kruse is evident in the style of this charming pair of dolls. They are both unmarked but the realistic detail suggests that they were probably sculptured and painted by a Berlin artist at the same time as the Munich Art Dolls (see p.37). Their velvet bodies and original clothes are in perfect condition and this together with their rarity means they will command a premium.
Height: 20in (50cm)
Value: $1,500-2,000 each

DOLL NAME	DATE	CHARACTERISTICS
Doll 1	1911	Wide body; legs with five seams head with three seams, sewn onto the body, painted face and hair.
Schlenkerchen	1922	The only smiling doll; head and limbs loosely sewn on and an open-closed mouth.
Du Mein	c.1925	Large, heavy baby with loosely attached head, open eyes, and weighted body. Also toddler version.
Traumerchen	c.1925	As Du Mein but with closed eyes.

Lenci

Enrico and Elena Scavini founded the Lenci firm in Turin in 1915 initially making decorative objects for the home. Its series of felt dolls was instantly popular and has remained so to this day. The first advertisement for Madame E. Scavini's dolls appears to have been issued in the American trade magazine *Playthings* in 1920. Beautifully designed and well-made, they are distinguished by their elaborate, stylish, and brightly-colored clothes.

Generally bought for display rather than as playthings, many of them have survived virtually unscathed, so value is strictly related to condition.

The most sought-after Lenci dolls are the early ones that were given painted wooden accessories, especially those figures modeled after a famous person, such as Rudolf Valentino elaborately dressed as the Sheik in the film of that name, and carrying a carved and painted wooden dagger and revolver (see p.15).

LEFT It is astonishing to see the variety of expressions Lenci managed to produce in its dolls' faces, yet all were unmistakably Lenci. This 1930s child from the 1500 series looks thoroughly bad-tempered and naughty, whereas many of its children had pretty, serene faces. She is wearing her original patchwork dress in characteristically bright colors and has a brown mohair wig. Other typical features include the side-glancing eyes and the joined together middle two fingers.
Height: 18in (45cm)
Value: $1,500-2,000

RIGHT Pierrot is one of the first dolls Lenci made, and is one of the dolls that appeared in the first advertisement. He was produced with a variety of expressions, but always sad and glancing sideways out of half-shut eyes. Typical of Lenci's early dolls, this one has a wooden accessory—in this case a mandolin—and the fact that this has survived will add to the value.
Height: 23in (59cm)
Value: $1,800-2,800

BELOW Early dolls from the 1920s and 1930s are usually stamped in purple or black on the foot, and this is often faded today. Others had a paper label such as the one shown here, taken from a 1920's Spanish dancer, attached to the clothes and printed with the name Lenci and the design number of the doll. Note the unusual Art Nouveau writing, probably used before the familiar Lenci script was registered as a trademark in 1919. Some dolls have a metal button attached, in a similar style to that used on Steiff dolls.

RIGHT This Dutch boy is one of the 300 series of dolls that were dressed in national costume. This boy is model 11; other dolls were dressed as Russian, Swedish, or Finnish children. Some dolls in the series were dressed in sporting costumes to resemble golfers, oarsmen, and football players. First made in 1929, these dolls had hollow felt bodies rather than stuffed ones.
Height: 17½in (44.5cm)
Value: $2,000–3,000

LEFT This group of Lencis includes dolls of various sizes and dates, but all are in their original clothes. Lenci arms are generally curved. Today, the joined two middle fingers are seen as a typical characteristic of Lencis, but as can be seen on the doll on the far left, sometimes the fingers were all joined.
Height (left to right): 149 series 16in (40.5cm); 450 series 13in (33cm); 109 series 22in (55cm); 450 series 13in (33cm)
Value: $500–1,200 each

J. K. Farnell

The firm of J. K. Farnell was founded in 1840 in Notting Hill, London, England, initially making pincushions, but soon moving on to soft toys. When its founder John died in 1897, his children Agnes and Henry moved to Acton in East London, where they started to produce soft toys, including their high-quality plush teddy bears. In 1925 they registered the Alpha trademark. As with the bears, the quality of design and execution of their dolls was consistently high. Some of their Alpha toys, especially their children, rival in beauty and quality those made by Lenci in Italy. Among the dolls Farnell produced is a series of musical dolls and a number of beautifully painted children dressed in high-quality clothing and reminiscent of the illustrations of Kate Greenaway.

Most Farnell dolls date from the 1930s. In 1935 the trademarks Alpha Cherub Dolls and Joy Day were registered. Farnell dolls are quite hard to find today, possibly because their production quantities were smaller than those of other manufacturers, but they are worth looking for because they add luster to any doll collection.

LEFT In the 1930s, Farnell produced a range of musical dolls dressed in the costumes of various countries; among them was this charming felt black mammy doll holding a tiny baby.
Height: 12in (30.5cm)
Value: $450–600

ABOVE "Ole Bill" is a rare and interesting early Farnell based on the First World War cartoon character created by Bruce Bainsfather. Patented in 1915, he is particularly interesting as a historical document as he is wearing the typical army uniform of the time. A 4¾in (12cm) version was also made.
Height: 18in (46cm)
Value: $450–600

ABOVE This doll was originally designed to represent Edward VIII, but after the King's abdication in 1937, Farnell re-issued the doll as George VI. Shown here in a Scot's Guard's uniform, the doll was also made wearing Coronation robes and Highland dress.
Height: 15in (38cm)
Value: $300–450

Dean's Rag Book Co. Ltd

Dean's Rag Book Co. Ltd was founded in 1903 by Henry Samuel Dean as a subsidiary of Dean and Son, a printing and publishing firm that had existed since the 18th century. They first made washable rag books designed for babies and illustrated with toys, animals, children, and cars. They also produced a range of rag books featuring various characters such as soldiers and postmen which could be cut out and made up into dolls at home. For an extra charge, the dolls could be bought already made. The first felt dolls were made in the 1920s with stiffened fabric faces; some based on characters from children's books.

Composition heads were made in the 1930s, followed by hard rubber at the end of the 1940s (see p.147).

ABOVE Dean's dolls were patented in 1908 and the soles of their feet were printed with this Dean's Rag Book logo of two dogs fighting over a rag book.

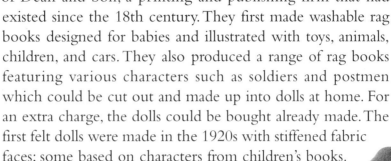

RIGHT Later Dean's dolls, like this Buffalo Billy from 1951, had painted rubber heads rather than the cloth ones of earlier examples. He is wearing his original cowboy clothes with art plush chaps and is in pristine condition. He was made to partner a friend called Annie.
Height: 15in (38cm)
Value: $400-600

ABOVE LEFT and RIGHT
Miss Betty Oxo was made by Dean's as a promotional gift for the famous beef cube and gravy firm of Oxo. The early example on the left, from c.1920, must have been very popular with consumers as she is still found in large quantities. With her intelligent wide-awake, molded, and painted face, and pretty velvet clothes

trimmed with art plush, it is easy to understand her appeal. The dolls were dressed in a variety of pastel-colored clothes which changed over the years. As with all cloth dolls, condition is all-important and the fact that this example is still fresh and bright will add to her value. By the 1930s Betty had changed into Little Miss Oxo,

with a cloth body and simple felt clothes. These later dolls are much rarer than the earlier ones but because of their lesser quality they fetch similar prices. They do not have the Dean's label, but "Oxo" is sewn on the dress pocket.
Height: left 20in (51cm); right 18in (46cm)
Value: left $500-700; right $400-600

Chad Valley

Set up in Birmingham in 1820 as a printing business by Joseph and Alfred Johnson, Johnson Bros. Ltd. became Chad Valley in 1897 when it moved to Harborne on the river Chad. In 1920 the factory moved again, to the Wrekin Toy Works in Shropshire, but retained the Chad Valley name as it was by now well-established in the toy business as a maker of high-quality teddy bears, puzzles, and games.

Chad Valley is unique, as it made toys of every kind and used a wide variety of materials, from tin, cloth, card, paper, felt, plush, and wood to hard plastic. Because of this, a Chad Valley collection would provide a very interesting overview of English toy-making in the 20th century.

The quality of Chad Valley's toys was so high that in 1938 they were granted a Royal Warrant of Appointment as Toymakers to Her Majesty the Queen; this warrant continued when Elizabeth II became Queen, and stayed with her as the Queen Mother—something which is very helpful when trying to date dolls. Today Chad is most famous for its toys based on popular characters, as well as the dolls representing Princess Elizabeth and Princess Margaret. In 1978 the company was taken over by Palitoy, and in 1988 the Woolworths chain adopted the name.

LEFT This delightful English nursery rhyme character, Little Bo Peep, has lost her sheep, and she even has painted tears rolling down her cheeks to show her distress. Other nursery characters by Chad Valley include a Little Boy Blue. Made in 1935, this Little Bo Peep still has all her original clothes and is in excellent condition.
Height: 14in (35.5cm)
Value: $400-600

RIGHT Chad Valley produced this first version of Princess Elizabeth in 1930 with the approval of her mother, the Duchess of York. It is based on a charming photograph of the 4-year-old princess in which she is wearing a similar layered organdy dress and pearl necklace. At the time it was made it was sold for one guinea at the express wish of her parents, who wanted it to be affordable to the populace. This doll is much rarer than the later, 1938 model, which was made as a pair with her sister Princess Margaret. The two girls were dressed in blue and pink felt coats and hats. Typically, this one has a stitched molded, velvet body and painted felt face.
Height: 17½in (46cm)
Value: $800-1,200

LEFT Chad Valley modeled many of its dolls on famous characters. This cheeky doll with her mischievous inset glass eyes was designed by English children's illustrator Mabel Lucie Attwell. Dressed in her original clothes and with an unusual auburn mohair wig, this example still has its original box, which doubled as a bed. These popular dolls were first made in 1927 in three sizes. Today they are among the most sought-after of Chad Valley's dolls, and this one, in excellent condition, is a fine example. The box bears the "CV" logo and the doll has a celluloid-covered metal button and a label.
Height: 12in (30.5cm)
Value: $800–1,200

Mabel Lucie Attwell box label

1930s embroidered label

1938–53 foot label
and chest tag

RIGHT Chad Valley made numerous versions of this delightful Snow White and the Seven Dwarfs set, varying the size of the dwarfs (either 9in/23cm or 7in/18cm) and the color of Snow White's dress. In a white dress—presumably for when she married Prince Charming—she is particularly hard to find. Also very rare is a musical set operated by keys. Appropriately, Snow White's tune was "One day my Prince will come!" All versions were made with swing tags and in boxes stamped with their individual name. Often, Snow White is in worse condition than the dwarfs, perhaps being irresistible as a play doll.
Height: Dwarfs 7in (18cm); Snow White 15in (38cm)
Value: $1,500–2,500 the set

Norah Wellings

Initially, Norah Wellings produced doll designs for other famous manufacturers including Chad Valley. In 1926 she set up her own soft toy business in Wellington, Shropshire, in partnership with her brother Leonard. Although she also made teddy bears, it is for her felt dolls that she is most famous today. All her dolls were her own designs and there is a definite family look to them. They all have swivel necks, and can often be recognised by the separately sewn-on ears. They were made in a variety of sizes and types, but perhaps most easy to find are the cheerful little sailor dolls that were sold to passengers on liners with the name of the ship on the hat band. Production ceased in 1960. Because they are easy to find and inexpensive, her dolls are very popular with collectors.

LEFT This charming little girl from 1938 is probably one of Norah Wellings' most desirable dolls. She has a well-painted felt face, mohair wig, and a very pretty Lenci-type organdy dress decorated with felt flowers. Even her fingers have been joined together, although not in quite the same manner as those of Lenci dolls (see pp.132-3). Height: 14½in (37cm) Value: $600-900

RIGHT This 1930s Admiral with his smiling face is very similar to the bell-buttoned sailor boys also made by Norah Wellings for the passenger liners. He has a brushed cotton painted face and a velvet tailed coat; the liner dolls wore all-in-one tunics and had flat caps. Height: 9½in (24cm) Value: $75-125

RIGHT It was fashionable from the 1930s to the 1950s to keep clean handkerchiefs or a nightgown in attractive bags which were often in the form of dolls or toys. This example, modeled as a gypsy, was made in 1938. Her skirt and matching scarf are of printed silk and her jacket is felt. Like many other Norah Wellings dolls, she has painted eyes. Height: 19in (48cm) Value: $200-350

Old Cottage Dolls

Old Cottage Dolls were made by Mrs Fleischmann and her daughter Suzanne, both Czech refugees working in England. They registered the name in 1948 and continued to make the dolls until the 1970s. Each doll had a swing tag with a picture of an old cottage on the reverse. Some later dolls carried the Design Center Award. Although the clothes were made to be removed, it would seem that little girls treasured them because today most examples that have survived are in good condition.

RIGHT and BELOW This group of delightful Old Cottage Dolls are typical examples and represent the two sizes produced. Their pretty hard plastic faces tend to warp, resulting in these rather lop-sided expressions. They have felt bodies and are always beautifully dressed, usually in historical costume or as characters such as Quaker girls. Rare examples of the pair's work include a toy marionette and a baby, both of which command a premium when they appear on the market. The small doll on the bottom left is dressed as Little Bo Peep; the one on the right is a Victorian Miss and was probably the most popular character they produced. The large doll on the right is unusual because she is dressed in 1950s-style clothes.
Height: large 10in (25.4cm); small 8in (20cm)
Value: large $150-300; small $125-175

Miscellaneous Cloth

Cloth dolls perhaps offer more scope than any other medium to the collector looking for rare or unusual pieces. Remember, though, that rarity does not equal value. Because you like a doll it does not necessarily follow that others will. But do not be deterred by low value if you find an interesting doll in good, clean condition that is well-made and attractive. Some cloth dolls have rocketed in value recently, although these are principally the well-dressed, pretty child dolls of the 1920s and 30s. Less expensive than the original Lenci and Käthe Kruse dolls are the many lookalikes made in France, Germany, and Italy. Although interesting, these are generally not as attractive as the originals and usually of poorer quality and collectors should be careful not to confuse them with the real thing.

RIGHT When Captain Scott and Roald Amundsen were exploring Antarctica in search of the South Pole in 1912, Eskimo dolls became very popular. This example, made in the 1920s, probably in England, comes complete with baby in papoose and is an amusing reminder of the time. Although of poor-quality felt and dual plush, the doll is in good condition.
Height: 9½in (24cm)
Value: $100-150

ABOVE Although only small, this doll is finely detailed. Her face is needle sculptured, with the nose pulled out by stitching and the other features embroidered on. Her fingers are separate and she has a human hair wig. She is wearing her original outfit with an elaborately wired and embroidered bodice over her linen blouse, a printed cotton skirt, and white kid boots. She is probably Middle European and possibly dates from the 1840s.
Height: 7½in (19cm)
Value: $300-500

RIGHT This knitted lady illustrates what fun it can be to collect dolls, even if you have only a limited budget. She is worth little as yet because little is known about her although this type of doll has been identified by the great authority Jane Coleman as being made by a cottage industry in New Brunswick, Canada, in the 1930s. The dolls have painted cotton faces and their bodies are wired so that they can be moved into different positions.
Height: 8in (20cm)
Value: $50-100

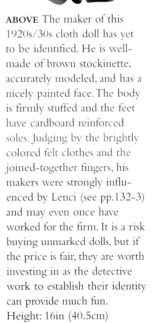

RIGHT This early 20th century English brown velvet-headed doll has colored plush clothes which are integral to his body. The ring on his chest suggests that he once carried a name tag, in a similar manner to the dolls made by a number of cloth doll manufacturers, such as Farnell and Dean's.
Height: 10½in (25.5cm)
Value: $150-300

ABOVE The maker of this 1920s/30s cloth doll has yet to be identified. He is well-made of brown stockinette, accurately modeled, and has a nicely painted face. The body is firmly stuffed and the feet have cardboard reinforced soles. Judging by the brightly colored felt clothes and the joined-together fingers, his makers were strongly influenced by Lenci (see pp.132-3) and may even once have worked for the firm. It is a risk buying unmarked dolls, but if the price is fair, they are worth investing in as the detective work to establish their identity can provide much fun.
Height: 16in (40.5cm)
Value: $200-400

ABOVE This funny little mascot doll was made by English doll and teddy bear maker, Merrythought, during the 1930s. She has a twisted metal thread loop in her crown to be used for hanging. The face is heat pressed and painted and is very similar in expression to Alpha Toy dolls' faces made by Farnell (see p.134)—many designers worked for more than one English manufacturer. The wool skirt, colored cotton beads, and red and black ribbons on her six tufts of hair are all original.
Height: 8in (20cm)
Value: $80-120

CELLULOID, PLASTIC, AND VINYL DOLLS

Celluloid has been used for dolls and dolls' heads in Germany since the 1890s and rubber dolls were made even earlier in the United States, but rubber in particular is easily perishable and few examples have survived in desirable condition. Hard plastic was introduced in dollmaking during the 1940s in the United States and a few years later in Britain. This durable material was a vast improvement over bisque or composition dolls as far as children were concerned, and firms such as Madame Alexander, Vogue, and Ideal began to upset the German monopoly on dolls held since the 1850s. A decade later vinyl was introduced. It is virtually unbreakable, soft to touch, and inexpensive, thus it is the main material for dolls today, with some new types of vinyl toys opening up new areas of collecting for the future.

Man-made materials carry their own problems and collectors should be aware of these: celluloid is highly flammable and cracks easily; rubber perishes and can crumble away; hard plastic is subject to a disease which causes it to blister and lose shape; and marks on vinyl are difficult to remove. However, these dolls can be rewarding to collect and are usually reasonably priced. But only buy dolls in good condition, in their original clothes, and with some attractive or unusual feature.

LEFT (left to right) A Pedigree vinyl Sindy, 1970s; a hard plastic walking Roddy doll, 1950s; a Mattel vinyl Barbie and Ken, 1980s; a late 1950s tudor rose baby, 1950s; and a hard plastic black Roddy, 1950s.

RIGHT A chemically hardened plaster Cupid made by the Lawton Doll Company in the 1920s.

Celluloid

Celluloid was invented in the 1870s and used for dolls by the 1890s. The main German maker was Rheinische Gummiund Celluloid Fabrik Co., founded in 1873 and famous for its turtle trademark that appears on the heads of dolls made over a long period and for many makers. Some of the celluloid dolls made before the First World War are very charming and full of detail despite their strange skin color. French celluloid dolls made during the inter-war years, usually representing plump, cheerful babies or toddlers, were well-designed. Most air-blown Japanese dolls are of poorer quality, but because of the charm of the designs, are becoming collectible.

ABOVE The celluloid face of this dwarf is crudely finished and his rabbit-skin beard and felt costume suggest he was made as a festive figure to accompany Father Christmas and his workers.
Height: 6⅓in (15cm)
Value: $35–75

RIGHT This dear little girl has the typical high color of the dolls produced by Rheinische Gummiund Celluloid Fabrik Co. in Germany. They made heads and parts for many firms including Kämmer & Reinhardt, Cuno and Otto Dressel, and Kestner. This 1930s doll was made by them for Bruno Schmidt of Waltershausen and has the firm's heart trade-mark with the initials "BSW" inside. She has a jointed composition body and is wearing a new dress.
Height: 18in (46cm)
Value: $300–450

RIGHT Film and book characters such as Charlie Chaplin and Billy Bunter command a premium because they are collected by film, comic, or Disney enthusiasts as well as by doll collectors. These air-blown hollow celluloid figures, impressed "made in Japan," date to the 1920s.
Height: left 7in (18cm); right 8in (20cm)
Value: $50-75 each

LEFT This dear little child figure, with a soulful expression and nicely molded clothes, is like many made in France, Germany, and Japan in the 1920s and 30s.
Height: 4in (10cm)
Value: $25-50

LEFT This French celluloid boy doll was produced by Petit Collin, one of the major manufacturers of celluloid dolls in France. He has nicely-molded hair and features, sleeping eyes, and a toddler body that can stand without support. Although this is a comparatively large doll, it is easy for a small child to carry round as it is so light. The limbs fit snugly to the torso and are easily moved to a new position. He would have been sold with pretty French baby doll clothes of the 1930s.
Height: 21in (53cm)
Value: $200-300

RIGHT The mark of French doll manufacturers Société Industrielle de Celluloid is one of the most common to be found on celluloid dolls. This baby from the 1930s has the typical jointed toddler body, painted, molded hair, and well-defined fingers and toes.
Height: 26in (66cm)
Value: $200-300

ABOVE The fact that this most unusual Japanese celluloid baby doll has the words "Baby Blue Eyes" impressed on the back of its head suggests it was made for the European market. The Fairylite trademark is found on many toys and even on pottery and was registered by Graham Brothers, a London importer. It is a very good quality doll and the modeling, especially of the body, owes a considerable amount to German bisque-headed baby dolls. The eyes, however, have no white highlights and the finger and toe nails are a curious shade of pink.
Height: 15in (38cm)
Value: $200-300

BELOW This inexpensive French celluloid-headed doll has a simple cloth body jointed with metal washers and pins and celluloid hands. When dressed the doll would be more appealing; she has deep blue glass eyes and an open/closed mouth with molded upper teeth.
Height: 8in (20cm)
Value: $50–75

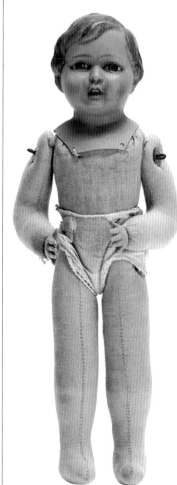

ABOVE It is interesting to compare these two dolls, as they were both probably made by the Rheinische Gummiund Celluloid Fabrik Co. in Germany, but the doll on the left is from the 1930s and the one on the right from the 1890s. They are Norwegian souvenir dolls. The oldest doll has curls molded over her forehead in the fashion of the time. She has disproportionately short bisque arms and a stuffed body. They show how a constant demand for these dolls was met by manufacturers producing a changing product over a number of years.
Height: left 12in (30.5cm); right 10in (25.4cm)
Value: left $75–125; right $100–150

Rubber, Plastic, and Vinyl

Apart from some rare mid-19th century American dolls with rubber heads, most rubber dolls are very affordable and should only be bought if they are in good condition or have some interesting feature. Many plastic dolls were made in the 1940s, but most popular today are American dolls, such as Vogue's small Ginnys and Madame Alexander's Alexanderkins, which can command high prices, particularly if still wearing their fine original outfits. Of the vinyl dolls introduced in the 1950s, the most collectible are Barbies. With most post-war dolls it is the variety of well-made costumes that most appeals to the collector, as they represent the styles and aspirations of the women and girls enjoying new prosperity after the austerity of the 1950s.

ABOVE This all-rubber doll made by William Goebel was designed by Berta Hummel, a German nun who is most famous for her little Goebel china figures of Bavarian children. These rubber dolls were made after the Second World War as a boy and a girl. This one is wearing his original Lederhosen, shirt, shoes, and socks, but has lost his hat.
Height: 12in (30.5cm)
Value: $90-120

ABOVE This 1950s Chad Valley doll, made under patent No. 517252, is of thin rubber over kapok, a soft yielding material suited to a baby and known as "magic skin." She is wearing her original rayon dress printed with rosebuds. Her simply-painted face is very baby-like with lightly molded features and curls around the temples. She is jointed at the neck, shoulders, and hips, although the head does not turn. She is in particularly good condition which will add to her value.
Height: 13½in (34cm)
Value: $90-120

ABOVE Dean's Rag Book Company (see p.135) produced this all-original rubber baby doll in the 1950s. Her face is beautifully molded and painted and she has shaded lustrous brown eyes, cherry red lips, and the palest of blond curls. Even her dress is attractive, decorated with a braid of embroidered Dutch figures. Rubber becomes brittle and is prone to cracking so great care has to be taken when handling these dolls today. However, despite the fragile nature of rubber, this doll has managed to survive in almost perfect condition.
Height: 18in (46cm)
Value: $350-450

ABOVE Madame Alexander was the tradename of Beatrice Behrman, who set up the Alexander Doll Company in 1923. She is probably the most famous doll maker in the United States and her dolls are eagerly sought-after by collectors of 20th century dolls. She is best-known for her plastic and vinyl dolls, which she produced from the 1940s onwards, but she also made dolls in cloth and composition in the 1920s and 1930s. As with the dolls of Jennie Graves on the facing page, the clothing is of very high quality and represents a high proportion of the doll's value. If it is tired, dirty or torn the doll is greatly devalued. Shown here are Amy, Meg, Beth, Jo Laurie, and Marmee, from Louisa May Alcott's novel, *Little Women*. With the exception of Laurie, who was part of the 755 series made only in 1967, they are all from the 781 series made between 1964 and 1971. Laurie and Marmee are standing on top of one of the boxes and from left to right are Amy, Meg, Beth, and Jo. Other sets by the company include members of the *The Sound of Music* family and characters from Peter Pan.
Height: 7½in (19cm) each
Value:$500–700 the set

RIGHT Also by Madame Alexander, this hard plastic Margot Ballerina is a little less flexible than the later vinyl-bodied ballerinas such as Elise. However, because she is earlier, 1953-55, she is harder to find and highly sought-after.
Height: 14in (35.5cm)
Value: $600–900

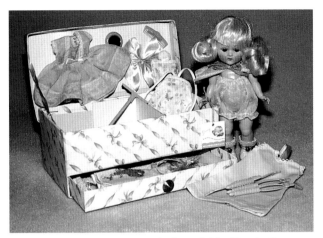

LEFT The American Character Doll Company was founded in 1919 in New York City, originally making all-composition dolls and in the 1920s and 1930s making "mama" dolls with cloth bodies and voice boxes. They produced this all-plastic Sweet Sue in 1953. Many wear gowns, but she appears as a dressy teenager.
Height: 18in (46cm)
Value: $200-350

ABOVE and BELOW Ginny was the brainchild of Jennie Graves, who first imported German dolls in 1922 to dress and sell in her Vogue Doll store. From 1937 to the 1940s (see p.41) the dolls were made in composition, and from 1948 Jennie started making them in hard plastic, first with painted eyes glancing to the side, but after 1950 with sleeping eyes. Later dolls had bendable knees and some walking examples were made. The earlier Ginnys are the most expensive to collect but all Ginnys are very collectible and those made in the 1940s and 1950s with their wealth of high quality costumes and accessories are particularly popular. Jennie Graves and later her daughter designed all the clothes and it is the attention to detail, the quality of the fabric, and the imaginative designs that make the dolls so desirable today. The doll above, made in 1952 in hard plastic, has brown sleeping eyes and comes complete with a fitted wardrobe chest full of clothes. Her tag reads "Wet, Combed, Curled, and Set" and has instructions on how to style her hair. The Ginny skater below, also from the 1950s, is a very rare doll.
Height: 8in (20cm) each
Value: above $900-1,400; below $600-800

LEFT The Arranbee Doll Company, founded in 1922, at first imported German bisque heads for its dolls, sometimes impressed with their name, the most notable being Armand Marseille's My Dream Baby (see p.109). This 1950s hard plastic Nancy Lee is wearing her original plaid evening gown.
Height: 17in (43cm)
Value: $300-500

RIGHT Rosebud was made by Eric and Hazel Smith of Northampton in the 1950s. Unlike her American counterpart, the British doll was not dressed in luxurious clothes because Britain had little money after the war and goods were in short supply. However these little dolls, especially in their original box, are historically interesting and appealing to collectors.
Height: 6in (15cm)
Value: $35-45

RIGHT Amanda Jane was
made in Hong Kong in the
1970s. She has rooted nylon
hair, painted features, and is
jointed at the neck and shoulders. She is wearing her original jeans and sweater but
unfortunately has spilled green
ink on her legs. She was also
made in a brown version and
as a baby with shorter hair
and a bent-limb body wearing
a sleeping suit.
Height: 6¾in (17cm)
Value: $15-25

ABOVE Patch, Sindy's sister,
was first produced by Mattel
in 1966 and portrays a typical
English girl with freckles and
none of the sophistication of
American Barbie's friend
Midge. Her original clothes of
kilt, jacket, and shirt were
popular with British girls in
the 1960s.
Height: 9in (23.5cm)
Value: $10-20

ABOVE Another inexpensive
1970s' vinyl doll is this Jenny,
dressed in her typically
English school uniform. She
has painted features, rooted,
slightly sparse coarse nylon
hair, and a ball neck joint that
allows her head to move
around in many positions. She
is a well-designed, attractive
doll but she has not managed
to maintain her value today.
Height: 7¼in (18.5cm)
Value: $10-20

LEFT Sasha Dolls were designed by Sasha Morgenthaler of
Switzerland in the 1940s. Early, extra large models are very rare,
as are the early Gotz manufactured dolls made between 1965
and 1969. These two were made by Trendon Toys Ltd of
Redditch, England, between 1965 and 1986. When Sasha
Morgenthaler died in 1975 the dolls became instantly collectible
as they were exceptionally well-made. They were made as a baby,
a white boy and girl called Sasha and Gregor and a black girl
and boy called Cora and Caleb. Gotz has recently reissued the
dolls and they can be bought in upscale toy stores.
Height: 16in (40.5cm) each
Value: $150-250 each; baby Sashas $75-150

ABOVE LEFT 1960s. Sindys in mint condition with their original boxes are rare but are well worth paying for. This original Sindy has the typically more childish figure of the early dolls, with flat feet; those of later dolls were molded to fit into high heels.
Height: 11in (28cm)
Value: $30–60

LEFT This vinyl Barbie-type doll made in Helsinki by K.E. Mathiasen in 1995 reflects the changes in Western culture. By pressing the side of her stomach a gentle swelling appears which if opened reveals twin babies!
Height: 12½in (31.75cm)
Value: $5–10

ABOVE Sindy was first made in 1962 by the Pedigree Doll Company and continued in production in virtually the same form until 1971 when she was remodeled to keep up with modern trends. The firm ceased making her in 1987 and Hasbro took over her manufacture, making this more up-to-date doll dressed in typical 1970s' clothes. The joy of collecting Sindy is that she is relatively easy to find at yard sales and flea markets as well as in charity stores. Look for dolls that are in good condition, are not stained, and whose clothes are fresh and plastic accessories not chipped.
Height: 12in (30.5cm)
Value: $12–20

ABOVE Hong Kong Lilli was brought out in imitation of Bild Lilli (right) between 1958 and 1960 to cash in on the craze for adult-looking fashion dolls. This example is wearing her original black bathing dress under her skirt ready for the beach and is complete with sun hat, towel, sandals, and beach bag. Although not a true Lilli, she is of interest to collectors of glamor dolls of the 1950s and 1960s because she is well-made, dressed in a appealing style, is in perfect condition in her original box, and is an unusually large size.
Height: 14½in (37cm)
Value: $50–100

ABOVE Bild Lilli was the doll Mattel's Barbie was based on (see right). Hamburg newspaper *Bild* ran a strip cartoon of a girl called Lilli and a doll was made in her image in Germany in the 1950s. She differs from Barbie in that she has painted earrings and shoes and a slightly slimmer figure. She originally came in a clear plastic case carrying a copy of the *Bild*. This Lilli has a crack on her shoulder which will detract from her value.
Height: 11in (28cm)
Value: $600–900

ABOVE Barbie was first made by Mattel in 1959. Her features have gradually changed and dolls made in the 1990s in China have gentler faces and more smiling mouths than earlier dolls. Barbie has today become a cult figure among collectors, many of whom avidly await the latest models to come out. This 1976 Toy Fair example is interesting, but even some new Barbies command a premium.
Height: 11½in (29cm)
Value: $120–180

RIGHT GI Joe was made by Hasbro between 1964 and 1976 in the United States. A controversial character, he was boycotted by some who opposed his representation of violence. He has gone through many changes, wearing different uniforms and moving from fighter to adventurer, and varying in size. The first dolls had painted hair and either brown or blue eyes and a scar on the right cheek. This group of 1960s dolls shows from left to right GI Joe dressed in Marine dress uniform, GI Joe as an AF test pilot and GI Joe dressed in marine fatigues.
Height: 12in (30.5cm) each
Value: $100-150

LEFT The Air Force Dress uniform of this 1980s GI Joe was produced in only very small numbers as children were more interested in his action suits. As a result he is very sought-after and rare today.
Height: 12in (30.5cm)
Value: $150-250

ABOVE GI Joe disappeared after the Vietnam War but returned as a miniature in the 1980s and was reissued in the original full size in the 1990s. These two represent Gung Ho and Rapid Fire.
Height: 12in (35.5cm) each
Value: $30-65

Dolls of Today

Choosing modern dolls is entirely personal, so buy what you like, and if others like it too, it may become collectible. There are two types of modern doll: expensive artist dolls and commercially available play dolls. If you fall in love with an expensive artist's doll be aware that there is no guarantee it will hold its value. You are paying for the artist's time and effort in producing a hand-made article. When buying modern play dolls, look for those that portray their period, as it is the sense of a time that is so fascinating about dolls; they should step right out of their age, whether it is the 1790s, 1890s, or 1990s. As with all dolls, their face is their fortune, and an interesting and appealing face will always be preferable to a run-of-the mill dolly face. Above all, look around and enjoy what is being made, whether in expensive limited editions, one-of-a-kind, or on the mass market. You don't have to have a niece or grand-daughter to pick a doll off a store shelf.

LEFT American doll and bear artist R. John Wright is one of the most successful artists working in the United States and one of the few whose dolls have appreciated in value during his lifetime. Much of his work is modeled on famous characters—he is well-known for his Winnie the Pooh bears—and this Little Prince from St Exupéray's children's story of that name is typical. As his label shows, he is number 78 in a limited edition of 250 dolls.
Height: 16½in (42cm)
Value: $2,500-3,500
(Cost in 1983: $425)

BELOW Modern play dolls are an interesting purchase, but only some hold their value and many in fact bring only a fraction of their original cost after a few years. The future collectibility of this 1996 Madame Alexander White Rabbit character from Lewis Carroll's *Alices Adventures in Wonderland* is difficult to ascertain, but Madame Alexander's dolls, especially these Alexanderkins first made in 1953, are highly regarded today.
Height: 7in (18cm)
Cost: $60

ABOVE One of the most revolutionary dolls to appear in 1996 was this Baby Expressions first marketed by Famosa in Spain in 1995. Battery-operated, it moves its face into a variety of expressions, laughing, crying, closing its eyes, and moving its arms! Only time will tell whether its expressions will continue to change as it ages!
Height: 15in (38cm)
Cost: $60-65

BELOW Among some of the best-quality baby dolls on the market today are those made in Germany by Zapf Creations in a vast variety of shapes and sizes, including a range of expensive porcelain dolls, and to suit every pocket. They are all well made and dressed in good-quality clothes. They also come with a great deal of information and provenance, and all the labels should be kept with the box if the doll is to retain its value or command a premium in the future. Milly shown here, is a soft bodied baby doll, one of the Colette range. She comes with a certificate of manufacture and a catalog of dolls' clothes she can wear.
Height:12in (30cm)
Cost: $60

ABOVE Baby dolls are always popular with collectors. Madame Alexander produced this baby Victoria in the early 1990s, although she has been made since the 1970s. She has a realistic baby face, cloth body, and vinyl limbs and although she is very pretty, it is likely that her 1970s sister will increase in value first.
Height: 18in (46cm)
Cost: $80

ABOVE Among high-quality modern dolls are those made by Corolle in France. Their Oriental baby doll Calin, which is described as having "Des attitudes de vrais bébés," and giving a child "L'experience d'une maman" won the Grand Prix du jouet affectif in 1995. Corolle also make dolls in larger sizes.
Height: 12in (30cm)
Cost: $60

ABOVE Often, black versions of dolls are more collectible than their white counterparts, possibly because they tend to be made in smaller quantities. Black Sindy dolls command up to one and a half times the price of white versions. The US-based Olmec company, which specializes in ethnic dolls, produced their Imani doll to personify many roles, including this dynamic singer, Sunshower. With her dreadlocks and bead jewelry, she reflects the Caribbean culture. Her features are similar to those of Barbie.
Height: 11½in (29cm)
Cost: (1996 version) $19.99

ABOVE Barbie doll exclusives have been produced for many stores throughout the world in limited numbers and are instantly appealing to the collector or tourist. Those from prestigious stores are apt to be more valuable in the future. Shown here is Hamley's West End Barbie, made in a limited edition of 25,000. On her box is a history of Hamley's which has been a major London toystore since its foundation in 1760 and was granted a Royal Warrant in 1938.
Height: 11½in (29cm)
Cost: $35

ABOVE Among collectible Barbies are those made in limited numbers or associated with film and television programs. This *Startrek* Barbie and Ken set was made to commemorate the 30th anniversary of the program in 1996.
Cost: $75   Height: 11½in (29cm)

ABOVE Dolls produced to mark important international events are popular with collectors, not only of dolls but of sporting memorabilia too. Shown here are a typical Barbie Olympic gymnast and a limited edition Cabbage Patch Olympikid, both made to commemorate the Olympic games held in Atlanta in the United States in 1996. Rare models of Cabbage Patch are among the few new dolls to fetch a higher secondary market value.
Height: Barbie 11½in (29cm); Cabbage Patch 14in (35.5cm)
Cost: Barbie $15; Cabbage Patch $25

RIGHT Lynne and Michael Roche from Bath, England, started making dolls based on bisque-headed German dolls and French bébés for people who could not afford the antiques. But by the 1980s their dolls were all their own original designs. Lynne designs the heads based on real children and designs the clothes, and Michael works on the molds, porcelain hands, and wooden or porcelain bodies. Their first models were made in 1982 and at least one new design and a special limited series are introduced each year, while some of the longer-standing designs are phased out. The very beautiful and highly-collectible dolls are all numbered, dated, and signed behind the left ear and on the torso. Shown here is Lillian, part of the 1997 collection, dressed in naturally dyed velvet and wool clothes.
Height: 20in (51cm)
Cost: $1,700

Paper Dolls

In the early 19th century English children's book publishers made paper dolls. By the 1840s French and German publishers started making boxed sets, sometimes with mahogany stands. When color printing became universal in the 1880s and 1890s printers, perhaps most famously Raphael Tuck, made paper dolls in series of ready-cut sets. Those made in the 20th century often represented famous people. Early ones were not an inexpensive alternative to real dolls as they were of very high quality, painted by highly-skilled craftsmen. Today, apart from these earliest dolls, prices are not punitive. When buying printed sheet dolls, uncut sheets are preferable to cut-out examples.

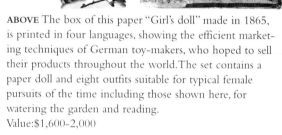

LEFT Jointed paper dolls such as this 1820s jester are known as Pantins, or Jumping Jacks. The faces were finely-painted in watercolors, but the clothes were colored in by a less skilled hand. The dolls were banned in France in the 18th century because they were alleged to frighten pregnant women so severely that they were in danger of miscarrying!
Value: $700-1,000 (a quarter of this if printed)

ABOVE The box of this paper "Girl's doll" made in 1865, is printed in four languages, showing the efficient marketing techniques of German toy-makers, who hoped to sell their products throughout the world. The set contains a paper doll and eight outfits suitable for typical female pursuits of the time including those shown here, for watering the garden and reading.
Value: $1,600-2,000

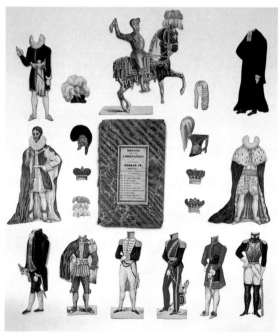

ABOVE It is rather curious that paper dolls printed and colored in Germany were known as "English dolls" (although some were made in England). These meticulously detailed examples from the 1780s, possibly made by H. F Müller, provide a perfect record of the fashions of the day, illustrating, among others, costumes for walking out, going to a masked ball, and bracing a winter's day.
Value: $2,500-3,500

RIGHT This rare hand-colored lithograph of a paper doll would have provided much fun for a young child. It was made for the coronation of George IV in July 1821, and it is still interesting today as a record of the people who attended the event. The coronation was particularly interesting as the King's wife, accused of adultery by her husband, was refused admittance.
Value: $2,500-3,500

Oddities

Many dolls' heads were made for purposes other than for play. Finding these can be an amusing pastime. A pull-along clockwork or hand-operated toy may often have a doll as part of it and these are usually great fun, especially if the dolls still have their original clothes. The *folie* or *marotte* is probably the most common "oddity," but others include dolls made from odd materials, such as corn husks, dried apples, rubber, metal, or even socks!

BELOW This amusing and unusual character doll, possibly by Hertel Schwab & Co., is actually a tea cosy. He has fine painted features and is wearing a lined and quilted leather coat and cap of the type worn for driving in a pre-First World War car.
Height: 12in (30.5cm)
Value: $800-1,200

RIGHT The Swiss firm of Bucherer produced a number of unusual metal dolls with ingenious ball joints that give them lots of flexibility. They used the trade name Saba in the 1920s. Many of them were modeled after famous characters including Charlie Chaplin.
Height: 8¾in (23cm)
Value: $150-400

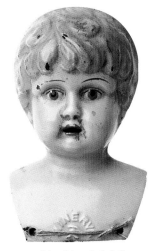

ABOVE When the bellows of this colorful toy-doll jester is pressed, he enthusiastically claps his symbols and squeaks. Advertised in the German toy catalogs of the 1920s, he has wire limbs and wooden hands and feet.
Height: 18in (46cm)
Value: $250-500

ABOVE Metal-headed dolls are uncommon but not highly prized. This painted tin one is stamped "Minerva," the trade name of the German manufacturers, Buschow & Beck. She has molded hair; others wore wigs. Brass and celluloid heads with the "Minerva" trademark were also made.
Height: 15½in (40cm)
Value: $100-250

Dolls' Tales

The background of a doll is always of interest because if known it helps put the doll into its historical and social context and can also help in dating and understanding other similar but unattributed dolls. It is a good idea to write down the history of your doll, if known, on a large label and attach it to a wrist or ankle. This particularly applies to dolls that are still, and will remain, in their original "families," as generations to come will be fascinated to know the doll they treasure belonged, for example, to their great grandmother who brought it over from Sweden with her when she married an English sea captain.

Victoria for the Red Cross

We do not know the early history of this beautiful French fashionable doll, only that she must have belonged to a very lucky and probably rich little girl, as not only does she have a very rare, high-quality jointed blown leather body, but she also possesses one of the largest wardrobes owned by a Paris doll in the 1870s. Dating from 1876, she has 69 articles of clothing, including 14 outfits, matching jewelry, and accessories.

During the dark days of the Second World War, Lady Alexander, whose family were great philanthropists in Faversham, Kent, England, donated Victoria to be raffled by the Red Cross. The tickets were sixpence (2½ new pence) each, and she was exhibited in a store window in the town wearing a different outfit each week. The winning ticket belonged to a little girl whose father worked for the railways. He was crushed to death while uncoupling two coaches one Christmas Eve. Although this brought great suffering to his wife and daughter, Victoria survived as a happy memory of him. She is now on display in a museum in Switzerland as a wonderful historical reminder of the fashions of her day.

Russians at Sea

This beautiful Jumeau doll with the distinctive heavy dark brows of the 1890s has an interesting history. She had been given as a leaving present to the governess of the Russian royal family by the daughters of the Duke and Duchess of Edinburgh who had themselves been given the doll as a souvenir when they stayed with their uncle

on his royal yacht. The Cyrillic script on the doll's hat band translates as "Roxanne," and the Lloyds' list, the daily list of shipping data and news produced since the 17th century by Lloyds of London, shows this as the name of the uncle's private yacht, built for him in Nantes in 1894. The boat was the ultimate in nautical luxury, and it even had electricity on board. On removing the doll's white summer cap covering, the enamel badge of the Russian Royal cypher was revealed on his hat band and can be seen in this picture.

Sophia's Bazzoni

Sophia Lloyd was born in 1847 and appears at the age of three or four, in the charming silhouette pictured below. She owned a very large wax doll which she looked after so well that nearly 150 years later it still looks as if it has just been unwrapped from its box. On the cloth body is a printed paper label with the words "A. Bazzoni maker." This doll's written documentation has made it possible to identify a number of other dolls which were previously unattributed, such as the doll on page 47.

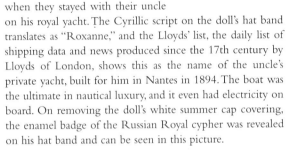

Sophy

This lovely Gaultier fashionable doll with a well jointed body by Gesland, was a present from Queen Victoria to her goddaughter, Princess Sophia, an Indian princess and daughter of the Maharaja Dulip Singh, who had been brought to England and raised under the Queen's guardianship.

It was a sumptuous present as the doll came with five changes of costume as well as accessories for her dressing table and for changes in the weather. Her black silk court train, which may be unique, was made in Paris to the exact specifications of the English court in the 1870s. Attached at the shoulders, it was made with a corner turned back showing the scarlet silk lining. This was because as a lady came out of a carriage an equerry would stand by with a baton to flip the train out of the way so that she wouldn't trip over it. Sophy also had a fabulous wedding dress with removable long sleeves and change of bodice, so it could be worn for balls, a traveling rug with leather straps, a muff, and a bone handled parasol.

Henrietta Berry

Henrietta belonged to Mary Jane Berry of Lynn, Massachusetts, who was born in April 1844 and died of consumption in 1855. She has been kept in her American family for five generations. She is wearing a wonderful wool dress and a professionally-made hat decorated with a red velvet ribbon and black feather which according to the owner's letter was made by a local milliner. She also has a cape, a prairie bonnet, bedding embroidered with the letters "HB," and a miniature book of poetry with a pencil-written note inside saying the book was given to Mary Jane by her brother, and which opens automatically onto a page of a Longfellow poem about remembrance. The diagonal eyelash painting is distinctive on this type of linen head, which appears occasionally. It was probably made by a small-scale New England manufacturer. Distinctive features include the wire frame around the shoulder plate and the lightweight body packed with sawdust. The shoes are beautifully made, and may well have been made by Mary Jane's father, who was registered as a shoemaker.

An English Miss in Scotland

This English dipped wax doll has an interesting provenance. Bought at a country house sale at Camperdown House outside Dundee in Scotland, she belonged to the third daughter of Admiral Viscount Duncan who lived between 1731 and 1804. Duncan was a great naval hero and contemporary of Nelson who had several Scottish Admirals in his fleet. He was famous not only for his bravery but for his enormous stature and good looks. Nelson was so fond of Duncan that on his death he wrote to his son that: "There is no man who more sincerely laments the heavy loss you have sustained than myself, but the name of Duncan will never be forgot by Britain, and in particular by its Navy, in which service the memory of your worthy father will, I am sure, grow up in you."

The sawdust stuffing has fallen out from the doll's pink kid arms but she still has her original early 19th century silk dress and hat and a trunk full of clothes, including caps, an ivory silk turban, a dark blue walking coat and muff in Hussars style, an organza evening dress with detachable long sleeves for day wear, a dressing gown, and a fashionable yellow silk gauze evening dress woven with silver thread. She not only represents an important time in history, but is also a perfect record of early 19th century fashions.

A Moroccan Lady

The parents of the owner of this doll went to Morocco with herself, her two sisters, and her brother in 1925 to try and cure her father's tuberculosis with the dry heat. One day she was invited for tea with her mother and sisters to a neighboring Harem, where her mother was presented with this wonderful doll dressed in a deep pink brocade with *djibbah* of white cotton, elaborate beaded head-dress, red velvet slippers decorated with metal braid, and a long white scarf falling down her back. The doll is an SFBJ mold 60 with short arms, sleeping dark eyes, and a brown mohair wig. Moroccan women had very little to occupy their time and a great amount of effort went into making cosmetics and doing embroidery. They were renowned for the wonderful clothes they made, which were of the finest material, worn in many layers, and finely embroidered. Although the doll by itself is of little interest, her clothes reflect the painstaking efforts of these women who lived in a sheltered world virtually locked away by their husbands. When the owner's father died two years after the doll was given to her in 1927, the doll was carefully put away and, protected from the light and dampness, she has survived in perfect condition today.

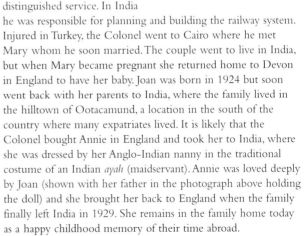

Annie

Annie is an attractive
Armand Marseille mold 390
black doll. The father of
Annie's owner Joan, was
Colonel Frederick R. H.
Eustace, R.E, who served in
the Royal Engineers in the
British Army in India
between 1900 and 1929 and
fought in France and with
General Allenby against
the Turks for which he
was awarded a DSO for
distinguished service. In India
he was responsible for planning and building the railway system.
Injured in Turkey, the Colonel went to Cairo where he met
Mary whom he soon married. The couple went to live in India,
but when Mary became pregnant she returned home to Devon
in England to have her baby. Joan was born in 1924 but soon
went back with her parents to India, where the family lived in
the hilltown of Ootacamund, a location in the south of the
country where many expatriates lived. It is likely that the
Colonel bought Annie in England and took her to India, where
she was dressed by her Anglo-Indian nanny in the traditional
costume of an Indian *ayah* (maidservant). Annie was loved deeply
by Joan (shown with her father in the photograph above holding
the doll) and she brought her back to England when the family
finally left India in 1929. She remains in the family home today
as a happy childhood memory of their time abroad.

A Widow's Story

This English turned wooden doll has had an interesting life. Her
elderly owner was called on by an antique dealer's scout who
offered her £20 ($30) for the doll. However, she rejected the
offer because of the doll's interesting history. The old lady had
been parlormaid to a clergyman's widow at the beginning of the
century and when she left to get married she was given the doll
by her mistress together with a manuscript about the doll's life.
The clergyman's wife was Jessie Challacombe and when her
husband died she had been forced to find a means of supporting
herself and her children and so began writing children's books
for the SPCK (Society for the Promotion of Christian
Knowledge), mainly on subjects of a moral nature. Among other
pieces, she wrote newspaper articles and a history of
Farnborough in Hampshire where she lived, but the most interesting is her hand-written story of the doll's life. Totally fictional,
it says that in 1910 the doll was 150 years old, although judging
by her quality and construction, it is more likely that the doll
was 100 years old at the time.

What is interesting about this story is that as long ago as the
beginning of the 20th century old dolls were already thought to
be special and their histories noteworthy.

Caring For Your Doll

Several things can damage dolls and their clothes and care should be taken to guard against these. Dirt will destroy fabrics and eat into some materials, making it impossible to remove. Dampness or moisture will loosen glue and joints, dissolve papier-mâché and composition, rust metal parts, and cause mold and rot. Heat will melt wax and create expansion cracks in composition and paint. Sunlight fades colors in silk, wool, cotton, and other fabrics and also creates rotting in silk. Moths attack wool and create holes and sometimes can destroy an entire outfit. Care has also to be taken to ward off mice, woodworm, and household pets.

Where you keep your doll is important. Make sure that as much dirt as possible is eliminated, that the doll is kept behind glass, or at least in a dust-free environment, away from sunlight, and in an even temperature and atmosphere that is not damp. But different materials require different conditions and the best thing is to consult a specialist, as an English carved wooden doll needs slightly more moisture in the atmosphere to preserve the gesso and paint than, say, a 20th century cloth doll.

Dolls should be kept in their original state whenever possible, as any addition or change will reduce the value. This means that you should try to keep the original wig, clothes, and accessories unless they are absolutely beyond repair. Obviously if you buy a doll with no clothes or hair, or one that is badly damaged or missing a limb, something should be done. Think seriously before undertaking any restoration: expert restorers are expensive, although the cost may be worth it. A rule of thumb to keep in mind is: if in doubt, don't. Often, you can disguise damage under clothes and hats and this may be preferable to a badly altered doll.

LEFT Dipped wax dolls are particularly susceptible to crazing and cracking, but the damage should be left alone. Some poured wax dolls can be restored, although only by a limited number of specialists who can do the job properly. This unusual little doll has a rare nodding and squeaking mechanism; but she has agreed so vociferously that her chest has broken! She has a lovely head with molded hair dipped in wax, and is worth careful repair because of her rarity and age. Don't rush into a job of this kind. Sometimes it is necessary to study a mechanism over several days before deciding on the best course of action, not only to replace the missing parts but to prevent the same damage from occurring again.

HAIR

Mohair and real hair wigs may become sparse and unkempt over the years through vigorous brushing by over-keen hands. Sometimes you may come across a doll that has lost its wig completely, but unless this is the case, it is best to try to keep the original hair rather than replace it, as a new wig will always lower the value of the doll. If the hair is sparse, try teasing it out gently; or cover it with a bonnet or hat. If the original really is beyond repair, it is important to make sure that any replacement is suitable for the style, coloring, and period of the doll. And always keep the original as a record. The best alternative to the original wig is an antique mohair replacement, although these are hard to find. Failing that, a new mohair wig can usually be bought from specialist stores. It may be difficult to find one that matches the doll exactly and sometimes a compromise will have to be made. Make sure that the wig is not too full for the doll's face. Man-made wigs should be avoided except on dolls made after the Second World War, when the original would have been man-made.

ABOVE The best alternative to the original wig is an antique replacement that suits the style of the doll. All this mohair wig needs is a few hairdressing techniques to tidy it up and give it back some curl. Seek professional help before attempting this, as brushing may pull out the mohair.

ABOVE This doll still has her original wig, although a previous owner has given her a short cut. When dressed in appropriate twenties' clothes the doll will probably look fine, and the shortened wig tells its own story of fashion and how children played with their dolls.

ABOVE This replacement wig is the correct material, being mohair, but it is rather too tightly curled, especially on top of the head. It is helpful to look at hairstyles in fashion magazines and children's books of the time; even old photographs can be of use when choosing a new style. A good quality wig such as this can then be dressed to look more suitable. This one is of a type popular with many collectors as it can be adapted to suit the period of the doll, and the fullness is an advantage as it allows for trimming.

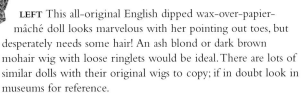

LEFT This all-original English dipped wax-over-papier-mâché doll looks marvelous with her pointing out toes, but desperately needs some hair! An ash blond or dark brown mohair wig with loose ringlets would be ideal. There are lots of similar dolls with their original wigs to copy; if in doubt look in museums for reference.

HEADS

If a bisque head is very badly damaged it may be worth replacing the head completely, particularly if the doll is relatively inexpensive. Firing cracks that occur during the firing process are not that worrisome, although they should be noted and the doll handled with particular care. Hairline cracks are more serious, although they can be stemmed by inserting a small amount of household glue along the line of the crack. Do not overpaint the crack as this will disfigure the doll, but clean it with a soap solution if there is dirt in it. The crack can then be disguised by pulling a hat down over it or combing the hair over the face. Serious damage to bisque and china should be dealt with by a specialist china restorer, but check that they give the right finish to the bisque. Ear chips should be left alone. Teeth can be replaced, but make sure they match the color of the original.

CLEANING DOLLS

Composition and papier-mâché dolls should not be washed, as the features were originally painted on in water soluble substances and will wash off. A light dusting may remove some of the excess grime, but otherwise you should leave well enough alone. Avoid cleaning wax dolls, too, as you may damage the wax surface or smudge the features. Be careful with composition as you may wipe off the varnish. Bisque and china can be washed using cotton balls dipped in soap and water, although try to avoid the eyes when working on the face. Surprisingly, cloth dolls do not lend themselves well to washing, even if a label on the doll claims it is washable, so any wet cleaning should be avoided; in some cases the task can be undertaken by a specialist professional cleaner.

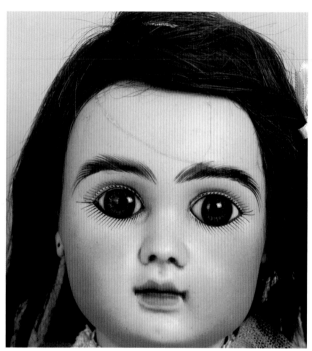

ABOVE and RIGHT Sadly, this pretty Steiner Figure A has been dropped, resulting in a crack in the forehead which can be seen in this close-up, above. The crack could be painted over by a professional porcelain restorer but in this case it has been thoroughly cleaned and covered by a new hairstyle, above right. Whichever way you decide to repair it, the value of the doll will be nowhere near that of an undamaged example. But it is interesting to note that some collectors today, unable to afford expensive perfect dolls, would rather buy a damaged example than not have one at all, even though the value will not increase to the same extent as that of a perfect doll.

EYES

If dolls have sleeping eyes they should be stored face down, not lying on their backs, as the eyes are held in position with dabs of plaster which will be weakened by the weight of the mechanism if the doll is on its back. Chips in the eyes can be left. Although dolls may look alarming if they are missing their eyes, this is one problem that can be solved relatively easily. Remove the pate to reveal the inside of the doll's head, where the eye mechanisms can be reached quite easily. Replacement eyes should match the color of the original and wherever possible should be glass not plastic. If eyelashes are missing, it is best to leave them alone rather than trying to find replacements.

RIGHT The pate has to be removed before any adjustments can be made to the eyes. Sometimes the glue has dried out and a

simple insertion between the bisque and papier-mâché circular dome should help. The original glues were either vegetable or animal and normally respond to light leverage or moistening. Kestner dolls have plaster pates which sometimes need more lengthy and careful treatment when removing them.

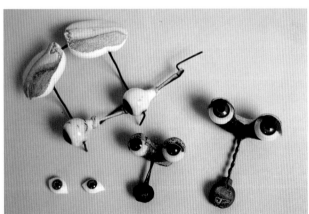

ABOVE Lozenge shaped eyes are used to create a permanent gaze and are found in most pre-1890 dolls. They are held in place by plaster and are the easiest to insert. The mechanism at the back of the picture is for flirty eyes, in which the eyeballs move from side to side in an amusing way. The two pairs of eyes on the right are for sleeping eyes, the weights falling back when the doll is laid down, "shutting" the eyes and revealing the pink lids.

BISQUE AND WOOD BODIES

Very often the jointed bodies of bisque dolls need re-stringing as the original elastic perishes over time. Be careful when handling such dolls as the head or limbs may fall off and break. Restringing should be done by a professional, although it can be done at home as there are books that explain the process. Beware of stringing a doll too tightly as the elastic may snap and may also weaken the sockets or even damage the bisque head. Stringing too loosely will cause the head to roll about unattractively. Special elastic and the correct tools must be used. Missing limbs can be disguised with clothes, or replacements found from old dolls. In the case of wood examples, new limbs can be made by a good carver, but note in the doll's history that this has been done. Do not overpaint fingers and toes; paint only the immediate area of repair and age it to match the color of the rest of the body.

RIGHT This simple baby's body is the easiest type to restring. The surrounding tools include string clamps, stringing hook, and sharp-nosed pliers. The paint has chipped from some parts of the body, showing the dark composition beneath. It is better to touch up the missing areas, rather than repaint the whole body.

RIGHT This type of body is more complicated to restring. It is a good idea to join a local or national doll club whose members are happy to share their experiences; alternatively there are classes where restringing and other simple repair work is taught.

CLOTH AND KID BODIES

Dolls with cloth or kid bodies can be repaired by restuffing with polyfill or sawdust (although sawdust can be harmful to leather) and carefully sewing up the slit, alternatively, a small patch may be necessary. Moth holes can be dealt with by patching the reverse of the material. Painted faces on cloth dolls should not be repainted as this will affect the value.

Dressing and Display

With some imagination even the least well-off collectors can make their display look attractive. It is tremendous fun looking for objects to enhance your doll and they are usually not expensive—a small toy for a character child, a miniature book for an adult, chairs, tables, washing sets, china food— can all be bought for your doll. Remember, dolls do not all have to stand up like soldiers on display stands. Why not have them in different positions, or sitting as a family group? There could be a hidden story—angry parents or a jealous girl—the ideas for display are limited only by your imagination. It is best if you try to keep everything to scale and don't mix your periods.

Great care should be taken to conserve the original dress of a doll as it forms an integral part of it and adds considerably to value. Only if a dress is well past hope should you think of replacing it; and then an antique alternative is preferable to a modern copy—look in specialist antique and doll shows, and at auctions of old baby clothes or old dolls' clothes; you will also find a wealth of accessories in these places. Try to dress the doll as closely to the original as possible, as there is nothing more ridiculous than a baby doll dressed as an adult or an adult dressed as a baby. If you do have to replace the clothes, take a photograph of the doll before you undress it.

RIGHT A fantastic accessory, this horse and gig go perfectly with this haughty French lady. She looks so imperious she is surely not offering anyone a ride, but with the whip in her hand she need have no fear that the horse will bolt.

ABOVE Stuffed animals are ideal to display with dolls. This group of Kämmer & Reinhardt dolls are playing with a Steiff "bully" dog. Keeping the dates and the nationality the same is always preferable to mixing them.

ABOVE These three happy children are playing with a German menagerie which may be slightly earlier than the German character dolls. However, the match is nice, and the dolls' expressive faces bring the whole scene to life.

LEFT The original owner of this Kämmer & Reinhardt mold 114 doll has fashioned it into a boy, cutting his hair into a page boy and clothing him in a simple, striped, front-buttoning, home-made dress typical of those worn by little boys at the start of the 20th century. To regain the original look for your doll go to doll museums for guidance; try to dress the doll in clothes of the period.

LEFT Clothes made for a doll during the first owner's childhood are always preferable to later additions, as they reflect the fashions of the period and often the techniques used. This mold 100 Kämmer & Reinhardt character doll is wearing contemporary Algerian knitted rompers made with a needle similar to a crochet hook.

LEFT Original babies' bonnets look marvelous on baby dolls. Don't forget to match the period, as even babies changed their fashions over the years. These examples are both early 20th century.

LEFT Shoes and boots are an important finishing touch. Again, study fashion styles to get the correct shoe design for your doll. Fit is often a problem, so carry an outline of your doll's foot at all times.

LEFT A selection of Victorian purses for dolls. It is very important to get the scale right for your doll. Imagine yourself with the accessory and see how big it is in relation to your hand, and apply the same scale to the doll.

Glossary

Applied ears Ears that are molded separately and applied to the head when it is removed from its mold.

Autoperipatetikos A clock-work mechanical walking doll patented in the United States in 1862.

Ball and hinge joint (or ball and tenon) A good quality joint found on wooden dolls.

Ball joint A ball-shaped joint used for articulating limbs, either as a loose ball between sections or attached to one part.

Bébé A French bisque-headed doll modeled to represent a young child rather than an adult.

Bébé tout en bois An all-wood baby doll made in Germany in the 1880s/90s.

Beeswax Natural wax from bees used for dolls' heads in the late 18th and early 19th centuries, often with a yellow tinge.

Bent-limb body A body with curved arms and legs without joints; usually found on baby dolls.

Bisque Unglazed porcelain.

Bonnet head A doll that has a molded bonnet or hat as part of its head.

Carton A mixture of card-board and composition, used for the bodies of French dolls and some early 19th century French heads.

Celluloid An inflammable man-made material of cel-lulose nitrate and camphor used for dolls from the 1890s.

Character dolls Dolls with realistic expressions.

Composition A mixture of wood pulp, plaster, and glue combined with a number of other materials including papier-mâché.

Crèche figures Religious figures made from wood, terracotta, and wax, most often representing charac-ters from the nativity.

Dipped wax A method for making dolls where an already painted papier-mâché head is dipped in molten wax.

Dolly face A stylized girl's face, usually with an open mouth and sleeping eyes.

Fashionable doll/Paris-ienne Bisque French lady dolls dressed in elaborate fashions, made from the 1860s to the early 20th century.

Flange neck A head type with a rounded base that fits into a hole in the body.

Flirty eyes Eyes that look from side to side.

Gesland body A stockinet body with padded wire arm-ature or internal framework made by Gesland and often found with a Gaultier head.

Gesso A mixture of plaster and size applied to wooden dolls as a base for paint.

Googly eyes Extremely large round eyes that glance to one side, made from 1911.

Grödnertals 19th century jointed wooden dolls made in the Gröden Valley.

Gutta percha A rubber substance derived from the coagulated milky latex of tropical trees, occasionally used to make the heads and bodies of dolls in the late 19th century.

Incised Usually used to refer to a maker's mark formed by a mold with raised letters making an impression in the clay.

Intaglio Concave eyes, which are either carved or molded, usually with painted pupils and irises.

Kapok A very light mater-ial used for stuffing dolls.

Kid Soft leather used for dolls' bodies from the early 19th century onwards.

Lady dolls *(see Fashionables)*

Masterbüchs German illus-trated catalogs produced to show a wholesaler's stock to buyers.

Open/closed mouth An open mouth, but without a hole through to the head.

Open mouth Doll with a mouth that is really open, rather than open/closed.

Papier-mâché A paper pulp made with glue that is then formed into a mold.

Pate A circular piece of cork, cardboard, or plaster covering the hole of some dolls' heads, and to which the wig is attached. Also sometimes used to refer to the top of a doll's head.

Peg woodens Wooden dolls with simple wooden peg joints and painted feet.

Poured bisque Liquid clay poured into a mold, allowed to solidify, and then poured off again.

Poured wax A method of making dolls where the wax is left to solidify in the mold and then poured out leaving a wax shell.

Pressed bisque Method of making early French bisque heads where clay is rolled out like pastry and pressed into a mold.

Pumpkin-head A German doll's head of papier-mâché dipped in wax, similar in shape to a pumpkin.

Shoulder head Head and shoulders in one piece.

Shoulder plate The part of the shoulder head below the head, sometimes as a separate piece.

Sleeping eyes Eyes that open and close.

Socket head A head that fits into a socket in the body, and can turn.

Stockinet A machine-knitted elastic fabric used for the bodies and some heads of dolls.

Stump dolls Crude English wooden dolls made in the 16th and 17th centuries, usually of oak.

Swivel head A head made separately from the shoul-der plate which can swivel.

Toddler body A baby body with straight legs, or a jointed toddler body with diagonally slanting hip joints and fat thighs.

Wax-over-composition A method of making wax dolls from the 1880s to 1920s where the inside is reinforced with plaster or composition.

Gazetteer

MUSEUMS

France

Musée des Arts Decoratifs
Palais du Louvre
107 rue de Rivoli
75001 Paris

Musée de la Poupée
Impasse Berthaud
(niveau 22 rue Beaubourg)
75003 Paris

Musée des Poupées
3 rue des Trente
51620 Josselin, Brittany

Germany

Coburger Puppenmuseum
Rückertstrasse 2
96450 Coburg

Deutches Spielzeugmuseum
Beethovenstrasse 10
96515 Sonneberg

Germanisches National
Museum
Kartäusergasse 1
90402 Nürnberg

Käthe Kruse
Puppenmuseum
Pflegstrasse 21a
86609 Donauwörth

Puppen und
Spielzeugmuseum
Hofbronnengasse 11-13
91541 Rothenburg/Tauber

Spielzeugmuseum der
Stadt, Nürnberg,
Karlstrasse no.13
90403 Nürnberg

Spielzeugmuseum im Alten
Rathausturm,
Marienplatz
80331 München

Great Britain

Bethnal Green Musuem of
Childhood
Cambridge Heath Road
London E2 9PA

London Toy and Model
Museum
21-3 Craven Hill
London W2 3EN

Museum of Childhood
42 High Street
Edinburgh
Lothian EH1 1TG

Warwick Doll Museum
Okens House
Castle Street
Warwick CV34 4BP

Japan

Yokohama Doll Museum
18 Yamashita-cho
Naka-ku
Yokohama, 231
Kanagawa-ken

Switzerland

Doll and Toy Museum
Promenade 83
CH-7270 Davos Platz

United States

Strong Musuem
One Manhattan Square
Rochester, NY 14607

Rosalie Whyel Museum of
Doll Art
1116 108th Avenue N.E.
Bellevue
Washington 98006

Wenham Historical
Association and Museum
132 Main Street
Wenham
Massachusetts 01984

Yesteryear's Museum
PO Box 609
Sandwich
Massachusetts 02563

AUCTION HOUSES

Christie's, South
Kensington
85 Old Brompton Road
London SW7 3LD

Sotheby's, London
34-5 New Bond Street
London W1A 2AA

Frasher's Doll Auctions Inc.
Rt 1 Box 142
Oak Grove
Missouri 64075

Theriault's, The Doll
Masters
PO Box 151
Anneapolis
MD 21404

DOLL CLUBS, MAGAZINES, AND ORGANIZATIONS

Australia

Australian Doll Digest
Box 680
Goulburn NSW 2580

France

Le Circle Privé de la
Poupée
47 rue Guersant
75017 Paris

Germany

Puppen und Spielzeug
Verlag Pur und Spielzeug
Postfach 101461,
47104 Duisburg
Stresemannstrasse 20-22

Great Britain

British Doll Collectors'
Club and News
"The Anchorage"
Wrotham Road
Culverstone
Meopham
Kent DA13 0QW

UK Doll Directory
Hugglets
PO Box 290
Brighton
East Sussex BN2 1DR

Spain

Miniaturas
Torre del Retiro
Av. Menendez Pelayo 67
28009 Madrid

United States

Antique Doll World
225 Main Street, Ste 300
Northport
New York 11768-9826

Contemporary Doll
Collector
Scott Publications
30595 Eight Mile
Livonia
Michegan 48152-1798

Doll Collectors of America
4 Bay Path Drive
Boylston
Massachusetts 01505

Dolls, The Collectors
Magazine
Collector Communications,
Inc.
170 Fifth Avenue
New York, NY 10010

Doll News
10920 North Ambassador
Drive
Kansas City
Missouri 64153

Doll Reader
Cumberland Publishing Inc.
6405 Flank Drive
Harrisburg
Pennsylvania 17112

Japanese American Doll
Enthusiasts
Baby Run Farm
1716 Baker Avenue
West Branch
Iowa 52358

National Antique Doll
Dealers' Association
c/o Jerome McGonagle
Box 323
Sudbury
Massachusetts 01776

United Federation of Doll
Clubs (UFDC)
10920 North Ambassador
Drive
Kansas City
Missouri 64153

Bibliography

The Blue Book
Jan Foulke
1995, Hobby House Press

**Care and Repair of
Antique and Modern
Dolls**
Faith Eaton
1985, BT Batsford Ltd.

Collecting Dolls
Nora Earnshaw
1987, Collins

**The Collector's
Encyclopedia of Dolls
Vols 1&2**
*Dorothy, Elizabeth & Evelyn
Coleman*
1986, Robert Hale

**The Collector's History
of Dolls**
Constance King
1977, Robert Hale

**Composition Dolls Vol 1
1928-55**
Polly and Pam Judd
1991, Hobby House Press

**Composition Dolls
Vol II 1909-28**
Polly and Pam Judd
1994, Hobby House Press

**The Dolls of Jules
Nicolas Steiner**
Dorothy A. McGonagle
1988, Hobby House Press

**The German Doll
Encylopedia 1800-1939**
Jürgen and Marianne Cieslik
1985, Hobby House Press

**The History of Wax
Dolls**
Mary Hillier
1985, Souvenir Press Ltd.

The Jumeau Book
*François Theimer & Florence
Theriault*
1994, Gold Horse Pubs.

**Kestner, King of Doll
Makers**
Jan Foulke
1982, Hobby House Press

Lenci
Sabine Reinelt
1990, Gert Wohlfarth
GmbH

Lenci Dolls
Dorothy S Coleman
1977, Hobby House Press

**The Letts Guide to
Collecting Dolls**
Kerry Taylor
1990, Studio Editions

**Miller's Antiques
Checklist: Dolls and
Teddy Bears**
Sue Pearson
1992, Mitchell Beazley

**Pollocks Dictionary of
English Dolls**
Mary Hillier, ed.
1982, Robert Hale Ltd.

**Pollocks History of
English Dolls and Toys**
K & M Fawdry
1979, Ernest Bonn

Simon & Halbig
Jan Foulke
1984, Hobby House Press

**Treasury of Käthe
Kruse Dolls**
Lydia Richter
1982, HP Books

**The Ultimate Doll
Book**
Caroline Goodfellow
1993, Dorling Kindersley

Understanding Dolls
Caroline Goodfellow
1983, Antique Collectors'
Club

World Guide to Dolls
Valerie Jackson Douet
1993, The Apple Press

Index

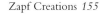

KEY

t top; b bottom; c centre; l left; r right

Photography

AC Andy Crawford

CSK Christie's South Kensington

DM Dorothy McGonagle

FB Frances Baird

GD Geoff Dann
(© De Agostini Editions)

H Hamleys

L&MR Lynne and Michael Roche

MP Michael Pearson
(© De Agostini Editions)

MW Michael Ward
(© De Agostini Editions)

SL Sotheby's, London

Collection

CO Carol Ohnemus

CSK Christie's South Kensington

DM Dorothy McGonagle

FB Frances Baird

HB Heather Bond

JK June P. Kibbe

JR Joan Robinson

LL Lorna Lieberman

L&MR Lynne and Michael Roche

MC Millie Caliri

MJ Marilyn Johnson

MP Maurine S. Popp

PK Phyllis Kransberg

RB Rosemarye Bunting

PC Private Collection

SB Stephen Buck

SL Sotheby's, London

SP Sue Pearson

PW Pam Walker

PZ Pam Zampiello

p.152/153/156/157 ©Mattel

p.151 ©Hasbro

While every effort has been made to credit every doll owner and photographer, and to trace the present copyright holders where relevant, we apologise in advance for any unintentional omission or error and will be pleased to insert the appropriate acknowledgment in any subsequent edition.

PICTURE CREDITS

6 CSK/CSK; **7** tl MW/CSK, br CSK/CSK; **8** tl GD/PC, tr CSK/CSK; **9** CSK/CSK; **10** CSK/CSK; **11** tl GD/PC; tr CSK/CSK; b MP/SP; **12** tl GD/CSK, b CSK; **13** t CSK/CSK, bl DM/MSP, br CSK/CSK; **14** tl DM/MSP, bl CSK/CSK, br MW/CSK; **15** tl MP/SP, tr MW/CSK, bl DM/DM, br CSK/CSK; **16** GD/PC; **17** tl CSK/CSK, br MW/CSK; **18** CSK/CSK; **19** CSK/CSK; **20** GD/PC; **21** l CSK/CSK, c PC, r GD/PC; **22** l CSK/CSK, r GD/PC, b PC; **23** l & c PC/GD, r CSK/CSK; **24** l DM/PZ, r DM/DM; **25** GD/PC; **26** GD/PC; **27** l GD/CSK, lc GD/PC, rc MW/CSK, r PC/GD; **28** GD/PC; **29** tl GD/PC, br CSK/CSK; **30** tl MW/CSK, bl GD/CSK, br CSK/CSK; **31** tl MW/CSK, tc GD/PC, tr GD/PC, b CSK/CSK; **32** l GD/CSK, tr GD/PC, br CSK/CSK; **33** l DM/MJ, r DM/MP; **34** DM/MP; **35** DM/MP; **36** PC/GD; **37** t GD/CSK; b GD/PC; **38** tl DM/MC, bl DM/DM, br GD/CSK; **39** tl DM/MC, tr DM/MC, bl DM/MC, bc DM/MC, br GD/PC; **40** t DM/MC, b DM/MJ; **41** tl DM/MC, tr GD/PC, bl DM/PZ, br DM/MC; **42** l GD/PC, r CSK/CSK; **43** l GD/PC, cl GD/PC, cr MP/PW, r MP/PW; **44** GD/PC; **45** tl CSK/CSK, br MW/CSK; **46** l CSK/CSK, c GD/PC, r CSK/CSK; **47** tl GD/PC, bl GD/PC, br CSK/CSK; **48** tl MP/SP, b CSK/CSK; **49** tl CSK/CSK, tr MP/HB, bl GD/CSK, br GD/PC; **50** tl GD/CSK, bl GD/PC, r GD/PC; **51** t GD/PC, bl CSK/CSK, br CSK/CSK; **52** GD/PC; **53** tl GD/PC, tr GD/CSK, bl MW/CSK, br MW/CSK; **54** GD/PC; **55** tl MW/CSK, br MW/CSK; **56** tl CSK/CSK, bl GD/PC, r CSK/MW; **57** tl CSK/CSK, tr GD/CSK, br MW/CSK; **58** bl GD/CSK, br MP/SP; **59** tr MW/CSK, b MW/CSK; **60** GD/PC; **61** tr GD/PC, cl CSK/CSK, bl MW/CSK, br GD/PC; **62** GD/PC; **63** GD/PC; **64** CSK/CSK; **65** tl CSK/CSK, cl MW/CSK, cr SL/SL, r MP/SP, bl DM/JK, cl MP/SP, c MP/SP, cr CSK/CSK, r SL/SL; **66** tr MW/CSK, bl CSK/CSK, br CSK/CSK; **67** tl CSK/CSK, bl CSK/CSK, r MW/CSK; **68** tl MP/SP, bl PC/GD, br CSK/CSK; **69** tl CSK/CSK, tr MP/SP, bl CSK/CSK, br GD/CSK; **70** l GD/PC, r CSK/CSK; **71** l CSK/CSK, c DM/DM, r DM/DM, tr DM/JK; **72** CSK/CSK; **73** tl MP/SP, tr MP/SP; b CSK/CSK; **74** l DM/DM, br GD/CSK; **75** tl CSK/CSK, bl MW/CSK, br CSK/CSK; **76** CSK/CSK; **77** CSK/CSK; **78** CSK/CSK; **79** tl GD/CSK, c CSK/CSK, tr CSK/CSK; **80** tl CSK/CSK, tr GD/CSK, b CSK/CSK; **81** tl CSK/CSK, tr MW/CSK, b MW/CSK; **82** tl GD/CSK, bl CSK/CSK, cr DM/DM, r DM/DM; **83** l CSK/CSK, c DM/DM, tr GD/CSK, bl CSK/CSK, bc CSK/CSK, br DM/DM; **84** tl DM/DM, tc DM/DM, tr CSK/CSK, bl DM/CO, br DM/DM; **85** tl DM/DM, tr DM/DM, bl GD/PC; **86** CSK/CSK; **87** CSK/CSK; **88** tl CSK/CSK, bc GD/CSK, br CSK/CSK; **89** tl CSK/CSK, tc GD/CSK, tr CSK/CSK, b CSK/CSK; **90** tl GD/CSK, bl CSK/CSK, br CSK/CSK; **91** tl MP/SP, tr MP/SP, b GD/CSK; **92** tl CSK/CSK, b GD/CSK; **93** l MW/CSK, c GD/CSK, r MW/GD; **94** l GD/CSK, r MW/CSK; **95** bl CSK/CSK, c MW/CSK, br MW/CSK; **96** tl GD/PC, br GD/CSK; **97** l GD/CSK, r MW/CSK; **98** t CSK/CSK, bl GD/PC, br MW/CSK; **99** l CSK/CSK, tr MP/SP; **100** CSK/CSK; **101** tl GD/CSK, tr MP/SP, bl CSK/CSK, br MP/SP; **102** tl GD/CSK, tr CSK/CSK, bl CSK/CSK, br CSK/CSK; **103** tl GD/CSK, tr GD/CSK, bl GD/CSK, br CSK/CSK; **104** l GD/CSK, tc CSK/CSK, c GD/CSK, r GD/CSK; **105** tl GD/CSK, tr GD/CSK, bl CSK/CSK, br MP/SP; **106** tl CSK/CSK, bl MP/HB, br MP/SP; **107** t CSK/CSK, bl GD/PC, br GD/PC; **108** tl MP/SP, bl GD/PC, br GD/PC; **109** t MP/SP, b GD/CSK; **110** tl MW/CSK, tr GD/CSK, bl MP/SP, br GD/CSK; **111** l MW/CSK, tr CSK/CSK, br MW/CSK; **112** tl GD/CSK, bl MW/CSK, br MW/CSK; **113** tl MW/CSK, tr & br GD/CSK, cl CSK/CSK, b MW/CSK; **114** t MW/CSK, cl MW/CSK, br MW/CSK; **115** tl MW/CSK, tc MW/CSK, tr CSK/CSK, bl GD/CSK, br MW/CSK; **116** tl CSK/CSK, tc GD/CSK, bl MW/CSK, bc MW/CSK; **117** tl MP/SP, tr MP/SP, bl GD/CSK, br MP/SP; **118** tl MW/CSK, tr MW/CSK, bl MW/CSK, bc MW/CSK; **119** tl MW/CSK, b GD/CSK, br MW/CSK; **120** GD/PC; **121** CSK/CSK; **122** DM/MP; **123** l DM/DM, c DM/MJ, r DM/DM; **124** tl DM/LL, bl DM/MJ, br MW/CSK; **125** tl DM/MJ, tlc DM/PK, trc DM/PK, tr DM/LL, bl GD/CSK, br MP/SP; **126** DM/MJ; **127** tl DM/RB, tr DM/MJ, bl DM/PK, bc DM/PK, br DM/PK; **128** CSK/CSK; **129** tl GD/PC, tr CSK/CSK, br GD/PC; **130** tl MW/CSK, bl CSK/CSK, bc GD/CSK, br MW/CSK; **131** tr CSK/CSK, b MW/CSK; **132** tl CSK/CSK, bl GD/CSK, r GD/CSK; **133** tCSK/CSK; **134** bl CSK/CSK, bc GD/CSK; **135** t MP/SP, bl MP/SP, bc GD/PC, br GD/PC; **136** tl MP/SP, bl GD/PC, br GD/PC; **137** CSK/CSK; **138** bl GD/PC, tr GD/PC, br GD/PC; **139** l GD/PC, bc GD/PC, br GD/PC; **140** GD/PC; **141** GD/PC, b CSK/CSK; **142** GD/PC; **143** tl DM/DM, br MP/PW; **144** tl GD/PC, bl GD/CSK, br MP/PW; **145** tl GD/PC, tr MP/PW, bl GD/PC, bc MP/SP, R GD/PC; **146** MW/CSK; **147** l GD/CSK, c GD/PC r GD/PC; **148** t DM/PZ, b DM/MC; **149** tl DM/DM, tr DM/MC, c DM/MC, bl DM/MC, br FB/FB; **150** tl GD/PC, bl MP/PW; **151** l FB/FB, tr GD/PC, bl GD/PC; **152** l GD/PC, c GD/CSK, r CSK/CSK; **153** DM/SB; **154** tl AC/H, bl DM/DM, br DM/DM; **155** t AC/H, bl DM/DM, c AC/H; br AC/H; **156** l AC/H, tr DM/DM, br DM/DM; **157** tl DM/DM, tc DM/DM, r L&MR/L&MR; **158** CSK/CSK; **159** CSK/CSK, c CSK/CSK, tr GD/CSK, br GD/CSK; **160** CSK/CSK; **161** CSK/CSK; **162** t DM/PZ, bl CSK/CSK, br GD/PC; **163** tl GD/PC; tr GD/JR; **164** GD/PC; **165** l GD/PC; cl MP/SP, cr MP/SP, r MP/SP; **166** MP/SP; **167** MP/SP; **168** MP/SP; **169** t CSK/CSK, cl GD/CSK, rc MP/SP, bl GD/CSK, br MP/SP

Author's Acknowledgments

My grateful thanks for help, encouragement, and above all friendship in the writing of this book go to Tim Bristol, Sue Cutbill, Barbara S. Day, Nora Earnshaw, Faith Eaton, John Gurney, Abi Holmes, Margot Kinciad, Alison Macfarlane, Dorothy McGonagle, Leyla Maniera, Polly Smith and Sylvia Thomas.

Publisher's Acknowledgments

The publishers would like to thank the following for their contribution to the book: Dorothy McGonagle (who would like to thank all her friends, especially Agnes Sura, who helped in ways innumerable), Sue and Michael Pearson, David Robinson, Eva Saltman at Hamley's, Christina Shuttleworth for compiling the index and Clare Shedden.